Dear Mom, I Hate You

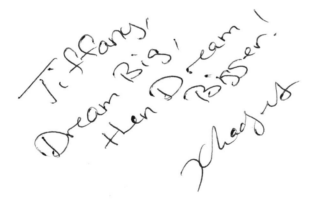

Khadija Grant

DEDICATIONS

Dear God, I just want to thank you.

To every character, setting, and plot twist in my life, I appreciate you; For it was you who made me who I am today.

To my mentors, Edwin "LIFE" Lawrence, Lawrence Wagner and Delia Busby, thank you for guiding me through my next chapter.

CHAPTER ONE

She called me. I didn't answer. She called me again.

I glanced at the movie screen, the images flashing before the audience. I watched their smiles, laughter and jaws chomping on buttered popcorn, all while licking salty crystals from their fingertips.

It rang. I still didn't answer.

"Who is it?" Kimani asked.

I sighed. "It's just my mother."

"Something wrong?"

I flipped the phone up and rolled my eyes. "Hey ma," I whispered.

"Hey, Dee. What you doing?"

Her voice was calm and cool, yet tinged with uncertainty.

"I'm at the movies, ma. What's up? Are my girls okay?"

"Yeah. We just left church. We're taking pictures tomorrow. I finally have all of my grandkids together!"

"Cool."

She went silent.

"Ma," I whispered, as I heard a few agitated voices in the theatre. "So everything is good?"

"Yes. My leg hurting a little bit, but I'm fine. You go on and watch your movie. Spend time with your husband. Call me when it's over."

"Okay."

A couple of days passed and I had yet to call her. I didn't call her back after the movies, I was too busy. I didn't call her the next day either, it skipped my mind, but she called me.

Her number blazed through the LED screen and it made me smile. She was always on time. If she hadn't heard my voice in a while, she'd pick up the phone and call to make sure I was okay. I wasn't okay. I had just spent the last couple of nights crying myself to sleep. Nightmares from my past were eating away at me and I had just confronted the most painful moment in my life. I needed to hear her voice.

I went into my father's house, smelling like barbecue ribs and steak fresh off the grill. My phone rang again. I answered it.

"Ma! I am so sorry I forgot —-"

"This is Malika," the voice said.

I looked at the number and then paused.

"Dee, your mother is dead. They are trying to resuscitate her."

Her words snatched the breath straight out of my body. My knees crashed down to the hardwood floor and I didn't feel a thing. My body went numb. I forgot where I was. I'd lost my mind.

"No!" I screamed, throwing my hands up.

I begged. I pleaded. "God please don't take my mother from me!"

"Khadija!" Kimani shouted. "Something wrong with the kids?"

"No!" I yelled.

My body trembled as if my soul escaped me.

"I can't take this!" I yelled.

I shook my head. I grabbed my chest. I screamed.

"What's going on?"

"My mother's dead! What am I going to do?"

"Get up!" Kimani said, pulling me off the floor.

He didn't give me a chance to think. I could barely see him through my teary eyes and I didn't have the strength to stand up, but he kept pulling at me.

"Where we going?" I asked, trying to understand his words.

"We're going to go see your mom."

I was confused. "But we don't have any money."

"We'll figure it out. Let's go!"

My father snatched his credit card from his wallet and placed it in Kimani's hand. We jumped into our Expedition, grabbed some mattress money and a book bag and was on the road within thirty minutes.

I couldn't control my breathing. I tried not to think about it. Her last words, "Call me back when the movie is over."

"But she loved me!" I yelled. "I let her down. I always let her down."

Suddenly, I could remember every little thing my mother did for me.

"Pat a cake. Pat a cake. Bakers man." It was the last moment I remembered spending with her. I could never forget her smile as she bounced my baby on her lap. She tapped my babies little feet, kissed her tiny fingers and smiled so big, it seemed she was having the time of her life. *"Roll it up and put it in the pan."* She laughed.

Just weeks before, I'd called her up in tears, desperate for some help. "Ma. Please can you take the girls for a little while —

"Of course! Bring my babies to me," she said, without hesitation. "I miss them so much and I'm going to take them to church because I know you're not going to do it."

3

It took us twelve hours to get from Cleveland to Jacksonville, North Carolina. I sat in her living room after the long drive, but was anxious to get up and go.

"Mom. I'm about to go to the mall," I told her. "I want to show Kimani around a bit."

My mother stopped bouncing my daughter and gave me the look. "But I wanted to spend time with you before you head back home," she said.

"I won't be gone long," I assured her.

That was a lie. I came back just thirty minutes before we had to get back on the road.

While sitting in the dark car as my husband sped through the mountains, I couldn't remember ever taking my mother out anywhere, just me and her. I never called her to just to say hello or to tell her how much she meant to me and when she sent me plant seeds for my sixteenth birthday, I shrugged it off. She said she wanted the plant to grow as I grew, but I threw them away.

"Khadija, calm down," Kimani said, as I began hyperventilating.

"I'm too young to lose my mother. I'm twenty years old! This is not fair! God! This is not fair! I want to die! I don't want to live anymore!"

"Your kids need you! Stop talking like that!"

"I don't fucking care! I need my mother!"

"Calm down, damn!" He turned to look at me as if I was a stranger, a wild woman feening for a drug, but when he saw the hurt and pain shrilling through my body, he took a deep breath, held my hand and said, "What did they say?"

My tears no longer coated my eyes as I cried. They were all dried out and itchy. I rocked back and forth in my seat and fought to breathe.

"She said my mother is dead and they are trying to bring her back."

"So she still alive?" he asked.

"Yes, but they said they don't think she gon' make it through the night."

He looked at me. He'd never seen me so weak. "You gonna just give up on her like that? Would she give up on you like that?"

CHAPTER TWO

We finally arrived in Greenville. My mother had been air-lifted two hours away from Jacksonville. Pitt Memorial Hospital was her only chance.

We walked into the hospital, asked for her name, and then was escorted to the ICU floor. I could smell tears in the air, hear the sounds of machines shoving life into the lifeless and hear random outbursts from tortured family members.

The ICU floor was like no other place on Earth. It was filled with mourning mothers, fathers and sisters and brothers. The floor felt eerie as I walked past still bodies barely clinging to life. The family members walked the halls like the walking dead and I wondered just how long it would take for me to turn, to lose myself. It took exactly ten steps, a glance at my mother lying still on the bed with a busted lip, tape holding down the plastic tubing cut into her throat. I lost it.

"Mommy!" I yelled.

My husband caught me in his arms. I couldn't remember the last time I'd called her that. The last time I longed to be in her arms.

I examined every machine hooked up to her body and listened to the sounds sustaining her. They were harsh sounds, beeping and pushing and pumping, but I was thankful for them.

"Don't give up on her," Kimani whispered, as I faltered to the ground.

"But you don't understand!"

"I don't," he agreed.

He looked at me and grabbed my arms as if he were going to shake me sane. "But, what you need to understand is that she needs you to be strong. How are you going to help her when you are falling out on the floor? I know for a fact your mother would be praying for you right now."

My sobbing stopped and I took in a deep breath. He was right. I'd given up. In my mind my mother was already dead. In my mind, I would never see my mother alive again. I wouldn't see her smile, feel her touch, her hug. If it were me clinging on to life, she would not be crying, she would be walking around my bed with blessed oil reciting every scripture of the bible. She would be…

I began to think about the many nights she'd sit with me and my brothers and sisters and read the Bible to us. We'd have our own bible study, fasting rituals and we'd watch biblical stories together.

One day during bible study, she opened up the palm of her hand. She said, "Khadija, What is this?"

I was only seven years old and had never seen anything like it. I nestled deeper into her lap and shrugged my shoulders.

"This is a mustard seed," she said. If you have faith the size of a mustard seed, you can do magical things. All you have to do is believe. That's it. It's really that simple."

I grabbed my mother's hand and kissed her cheeks. "I can do all things through Christ who strengthens me," I whispered in her ear.

I began to recite the scripture in my mind and the more I said it, the easier it was to breathe.

One day on the ICU floor turned into two. Two days turned into two weeks and before I knew it we were homeless, brushing our teeth and washing up in the ICU bathrooms before the morning nurses could kick us out.

"What happened?" I said to my mother's friend.

I wanted to back track. I needed to know every little detail. "I heard she was on the phone with you when she had the heart attack."

"She was about to go to church, but she called me," her friend said. "She needed to talk to me about something. She felt a pain in her chest, so she put the baby down. All I heard after that was the phone drop. I called 911, but they didn't get there fast enough. My son found her first and did CPR. He said when he got there, her tongue was purple and hanging from her mouth, but he kept doing CPR until the ambulance arrived."

Listening to her words in great detail made me imagine my mother alone, dying on the floor with no one to help her. But I still felt like there was something I could have done. I was in another state, but I wanted to know that I did all I could do.

I leaned in closer to her and said, "What do you think happened?"

She looked at me and turned away.

"What? What happened?" I begged.

"Your mother didn't want ya'll to know. She didn't want ya'll to carry her burden."

I was on the edge of my seat, ready to jump down her throat to snatch the words straight from her mouth.

"Your mother was trying to get the full-time position at work. She was waiting for weeks. She needed it. And she would have gotten it next week."

I took a deep breath. "So, she was worried about money?"

All I could think about was how ungrateful I was. I was so worried about myself, putting my kids off on her and she was stressed out about money.

"No. She needed full-time to get insurance. She needed her blood pressure pills, but couldn't afford her medication."

I was such in awe, I almost fell out my chair. I had no more questions, just guilt eating away at me. *I had forgotten. I had forgotten what I had vowed I'd do when I grew up. I failed her. I should have listened. I should have gone to college. If I had gone to college, I'd be able to afford what she needed.*

As I looked into my mother's empty eyes, I thought about her sacrifice and what I did with her investment. The many hours she worked so I could be healthy. The money she spent trying to get me to school on time so I could get a good education. I took it all for granted and she was lying there and there was nothing I could do for her.

When it came down to it, I couldn't convince the doctors that we had money, because we didn't. Wouldn't they treat her differently if I did? Try a little harder to bring my mother back?

Best believe it wouldn't happen again. I vowed I'd stay up all day and night and I would take good care of my mother. I would become a nurse, just like I promised her.

A group of doctors and medical students marched into the room. Some looked as if they had been up all night, while others were overly anxious to study a comatose patient. I stepped to the side.

"Dorothy, can you hear me?" One said. He turned to the students. "This is Dorothy and she is a 47 year old female suffering from a massive heart attack. Due to anoxia, tests show an absence of brain activity. She has a ten percent chance of surviving."

My heart dropped into my stomach. "What? She has no brain activity?"

The doctor turned toward me. "Are you her daughter?"

"Yes," I quickly said.

"There really isn't much we can do at this point. We completed a blood transfusion, placed a stint in her heart, but it's not looking good."

"But you have to do something!" I begged.

"We are doing all we can do. However, we need to start considering the facts. It is highly likely that we will have to remove her from the ventilator or life support soon."

I cried silent tears and held her hand as they walked out.

If only I could feel my phone vibrating again, I would answer it. I would tell her how much I loved her and how much I appreciated her, but it was too late. I would give anything in the world to see her smile again. I called her voicemail a thousand times hoping she would answer, but only her recorded voice greeted me and then she went away with a beep.

I begged God for just one more chance. I would get my life together so I could help her.

I looked at my mother as I shoved down the loud scream brewing in my chest.

I'M SORRY, MOM. I AM SO SORRY.

But, it was too late.

CHAPTER THREE

Even as a child, I was relentless. My mother called it faith. She instilled it in me that if I just had faith the size of a mustard seed, I could get whatever I wanted in life. So, I believed. I believed that someday, I would be freed from her strict regime. I believed that if having faith the size of a mustard seed could bring me toys, candy, and money, then it required faith the size of a basketball to get what I really wanted—to live with my father. It was going to take God and a miracle for her to let me go. It would prove to be the birth of a relentless spirit, flaming throughout my life.

The flame had struck in the late 1980s. It was the day my mother handed me the telephone. I was five years old when I did what she asked. I held the phone up to my little ear, smiled, and said, "Hello."

He didn't answer.

I stood in the kitchen wearing my Tom and Jerry pajamas while my brother played my turn on Super Mario Brothers. He was cheating. He was *always* cheating. He would run straight into the diamond roaches on purpose, so I could get eaten and jump short of the gaping hole. He wore a smirk each and every time. But when it was his turn, he didn't miss a beat. He'd bash the duck's shell for a hundred extra men, race the intense music up the brick steps, and swing on the flag as if he'd saved the day.

"Khadija," the man said. "Do you know who this is?"

I spun myself around the long spiral cord, wrapping my tiny body into an imaginary cocoon. I tugged at my hair bow and shrugged my shoulders.

"I don't know."

"This is your father," he said.

"My dad?"

My jaw dropped and my heart beat faster. I was witnessing a miracle. Something I'd never heard of before.

"But my daddy is in his room. My daddy just— "

"Yes, I am, Khadija. I'm your real father."

At that moment, I knew anything was possible. If I could have two fathers, then God must have been real. He definitely parted the Red Sea like I learned in Sunday school and he fed thousands with two loaves of bread and five small fish. That meant we would never be without bread and milk again. We would never have to use candles for light or the oven for heat, and my mother wouldn't become stressed every time she checked the mailbox.

God was magical and that was why my mother smeared blessed oil on my head every day before school, on every wall of the house at night, and on my brother's thieving hands. God was real. Not that I ever doubted Him before, but this was proof that anything was possible and I, being God's faithful daughter, I had the power to be a little magical, too.

It didn't take long for me to make our relationship official. I was seven years old when I walked my little tail down the altar, jumped into the cold, sanctified water, and was baptized in the name of Jesus.

"Hal-le-lujah!" My mother bawled, with the rest of the singers in the choir stand.

She ran up and down the pew, jumped up in the air, and had tears streaming down her cheeks. I worried about her sometimes. She'd shout, moving her feet to the beat, running into pews and stepping on people's toes. But shouting was something I could never do. I'd tried hundreds of times to imitate her, but my feet wouldn't move fast enough. She'd received the gift of the Holy Ghost. It was the gift that

"Khadija," she said, waving for me to hurry up.

"Yes," I said.

I stared down at her stockings. I was always checking my tone and looking at the ground, which helped me with my wandering eyes. If I looked too far to the right, left, or upward, I was being disrespectful. I wanted to keep my eyes, so I looked down.

"Look at me," she said.

I eased my head up. She was such a beautiful woman. She was 5'5" and petite, with long black curls that nestled around her neck. Her skin was caramel-colored and she had a small nose and medium-sized lips. She didn't have a big booty or big breasts like the other Southern mothers, but she could cook like one: Fried chicken, fried cabbage with a sliver of pork fatback, and some sweet cornbread that kept you from begging for seconds. She wore a long blue skirt that barely missed the concrete and a long-sleeved white blouse tucked tightly into her waistband. Her blouse buttoned all the way up to her neck and her eye color turned root beer under the rays of the sun. She didn't wear makeup or earrings and the only jewelry on her body was her wedding ring, but that was what made her so alluring.

I jumped in the car with my brothers and sisters, waved goodbye to my friends, and rocked to the music of John P. Kee.

My mother grabbed my hand. It was the hand with the Skittles. "If I see you hugging up on another man, I'm gonna beat the mess out of you," she leaned in to whisper.

I chewed slowly, savoring the flavor of the fruity Skittles, just in case she decided to smack them out my mouth.

"Okay," I said.

I'd heard it before. I just didn't understand how a Christian man, who smiled every time he saw me, would harm me. *It was just a hug.*

"Just wait 'til we get home," she said.

We hadn't even made it down the street before tears welled up in my eyes. I spoke to each traffic light as if I were psychic, begging them to take much longer to turn green. I watched as we passed house after house until finally getting to Sandy Run Apartments, my home.

Sandy Run was a community of about twenty, two-story, red brick buildings. Each complex was home to eight low-income families across many acres of land. My apartment was in the rear, where all the action went down. It was downstairs and under a solid metal staircase, the perfect place to sell drugs and plot your next move. We'd always joke about the name. "Sandy!" We'd shout out the school bus window. "Sandy Run!"

It was the hood. It was the ghetto, and although the police built a headquarters smack dab in the middle of the community, it was home, and I was never afraid of it. I was more afraid of the whipping my mother was about to give me.

Our driver pulled into our apartment parking lot and stopped. "Jesus!" she yelled.

Growing up, when an elder said "Jesus" with depth, as if truly calling for Him, I knew something was wrong.

Just a year before, my mother said "Jesus" three times in a row. It was a rainy night and my mother and stepfather would not stop arguing. She constantly warned him to stop driving like a bat out of hell, but he wouldn't listen. My stepfather drove like an amateur race car driver. He weaved in and out of traffic, doing his normal forty over the speed limit and riding the backs of any car that wouldn't move out of the way. I always felt safe with him, but that night was different. We almost died. We whipped past the other cars so fast, they disappeared. It was a game to him and a thrill ride for us kids, but we couldn't see a thing. Then something happened and for the first time, I saw fear surge through his body. He jammed on the brakes, causing the car to spin around three times, as my mother screamed from the top of her lungs, "Jesus! Jesus!" The car lifted off the ground, sliding across the highway until finally throwing us across the street into oncoming traffic. All I could hear were horns, tires screeching, and my mother screaming. I covered my ears. I closed my eyes. "Jesus," she said, one last time. The car immediately stopped, and everything got quiet. I opened my eyes. We were safe. As my mother would say, we were covered by the blood that night. Jesus seemed to always come on time.

There were so many people standing around our apartment building, we could barely see the stairway. There were kids jumping on a mattress by the dumpster, while their parents moved in to see what was going on. There weren't any police. There were never police around when you needed them. And then came the screams—screams that echoed off the metal steps and through the narrow hallway. The agony of her voice pierced my little heart.

The driver eased forward, stopping by the curb.

I cringed. I could feel something in the pit of my stomach.

My mother jumped out of the car. She called my sister's name. She pushed her way through the crowd. They didn't stop her. I wanted a man—any man—to help her. This wasn't her battle. Yet, they stood there, standing by the code. It was none of their business, but their business to watch.

"Mommy!"

I didn't want her to get hurt, but I was afraid, too. Everyone were staring at us. There we were, in long dresses, long-sleeved shirts covering most of our bodies, Bibles in our hands, yet we were still humans. We were the same Christians witnessing to our neighbors and begging them to get saved. But we were still humans. Humans with problems. Humans with pain.

19

I picked up the paper bag my mother dropped and swooped up the canned goods and oranges rolling down the street. My mother would be happy I did. At least I was good for something.

"No! Stop it!"

I tried to focus my eyes on where the shouting and screaming was coming from, but it was too dark, and I was too short.

"Was that your sister?" A neighbor said. "Damn. That's fucked up."

My stomach twisted tighter, squeezing nausea up my throat.

Is my sister okay? Is she in trouble?

Suddenly, I didn't care about a whipping. I didn't care if my mother beat me half to death, as long as my sister was okay.

I eased my way into the hallway that led to our apartment. I opened the screen door. My breath escaped me. The living room table was flipped upside-down and the couch was pushed across the room.

"I gotta get out of here," she kept saying.

I turned to look at her. It was my sister. She was okay.

I wanted so badly to tell her not to leave. To stay with me. I loved her. I didn't want to see her go. She was fourteen and I looked up to her. She would sneak me out of the house and take me places, like Golden Corral, where I could stuff as many gummy bears in my pocket as I wanted, walk out, and she wouldn't even tell Mommy. She would get up and make me eggs and toast in the morning. She stood up for herself and others. *Who will stand up for us now?*

"I'm outta here!" she cried hysterically.

I could hear my mother and stepfather yelling through their bedroom door. I looked at my sister. Her face was bloody as she paced back and forth, fighting the air with her fist. She wasn't scared of him. She was my hero.

All of a sudden, the bedroom door swung open. It was my stepfather.

I looked at my sister. She didn't move, but her eyes cut right through him.

He looked at her and walked out of the house.

"Go to your room, Khadija," my mother said.

I glanced at my sister to make sure she was okay, studying her torn clothes and busted lip. I took my little brother's hand and led him into the bedroom.

"Why?" my sister said. "Why won't you just leave him?"

"You know you're not supposed to be hanging out with them boys!" my mother yelled back. "If you just do what I tell you to do…"

"You don't get it, Mom!"

I'd never seen such betrayal in someone's eyes.

"You gon' just let him do me like that?" My sister said.

I heard a door slam and my mother talking to God again. I closed my teary eyes and I prayed, too. Maybe if we both talk to Him, He would listen. Maybe He could make a special trip for us both. "Dear God," I prayed. "I just want my mom to be happy."

CHAPTER FOUR

I'd only slept a couple of hours before my mother came whipping my blanket in the air. "Get up, Khadija. It's time for school."

She had a smile on her face, as if nothing had ever happened. I could hear the soulful voices of the Mississippi Mass Choir playing throughout the house, and my mother praising and praying while ironing her clothes.

I rushed into the bathroom. I needed to at least brush my teeth before my big sister came barging in to kick me out. But as I closed the door, I remembered. She wasn't there.

I sat down with my younger brother and sister and took a bite out of my maple-flavored sausage patty. I swallowed down hurt and confusion along with my buttered, flaky biscuits. I was becoming a pro at it. I'd mastered it. Every question I had, I answered it as logically as a child could.

Maybe he doesn't like us anymore. Maybe he wishes we weren't here.

There was no one there to stop me from fantasizing the worst. No one there to comfort my nagging worries or assure me that everything was all right. My problems didn't matter enough; I was just a kid living in an adult's world. But I saw what they saw. I heard loud and clear their worries about money, bills, and the yelling and fighting. I just couldn't understand it. I stayed in a child's place and watched them live in theirs.

I stuffed the last piece of sausage down my throat and snatched up my book bag. I wasn't missing the bus for anything. The last time the bus left me, my mom threw some keys at my head and threatened me with my brother's drumsticks. From then on, I was an on-time girl.

I stood at the bus stop, shivering, while the kids chose me as their entertainment. "Ain't you cold, Khadija?"

"No," I said, biting down on the quiver in my voice. I pulled my oversized coat tighter, but the drift of icy wind always made its way up my dress. The other kids at the bus stop wore pants—jeans, even. They rocked the latest Jordans and always had the nicest Triple Fat Goose and Tommy Hilfiger.

The children had a ball teasing me and hassling me with questions. "Why do you always dress like you are going to church?"

I had always replied with, "I'm Christian."

They would say, "Well, I am too," and then the awkward feeling and teasing would begin. It was difficult to explain and even more difficult to live. I would walk the halls of my school with my head held down and eat lunch by myself. Even some kids who went to my church would avoid me. This was the first time I realized that it wasn't my clothes that made me stand out or made them think I was weird. Maybe it was something else. I'd wear big, heavy coats to cover up my shameful body parts. Anything to not attract attention. But that day, attention was something I couldn't avoid.

I didn't have the answers to their questions and worse, I didn't have the courage to speak up, to make them stop. No matter how many times the little voice in my head told me to just say it—to just tell them to leave me alone—I couldn't.

Finally, the bus came and saved me from a fight and frostbite. I sat as close to the bus driver as possible. I could hear the other kids cussing and jumping over seats like they were at the playground. They were *so* going to Hell.

"Shut up and sit down!" the driver yelled. "If ya'll were my kids, I'd whip you 'til you turned blue," he mumbled. "Then I'd beat ya'll bad asses some mo'."

"Ooooh, he cussed!" one boy shouted.

The kids erupted in laughter. They either ignored him or cussed back, but me, I looked out the window and studied the beautiful houses. The homes with a swimming pool on the side, large windows, and even ones with their own porch. Sometimes, I would see people walking their well-groomed dogs or jogging through the neighborhood.

My favorite part of the ride was when we had to stop at a stop sign or a traffic light and I could get an even better glimpse of the life outside my gated community. I would push my toes against the bottom of the seat and lift up as high as I could to see the inside of their living rooms. They always seemed to have two tables: One that was dressed in silky cloth with huge wooden chairs that had beautiful engraved designs on them, and another that was plain like ours.

The homes that looked like mansions gave me hope. One day, I would buy my mother one of those houses and I would have my own room and a dog to guard the house. And the closer we got to the school, the bigger the homes grew and the bigger my dreams became. They were mostly owned by white families with their beautiful landscaped yards. It seemed the black families were cast away behind the gate of the warning sign, "SANDY RUN" —far, far away from them.

At school, I sat in the front row, right where I could be groomed as the teacher's pet. "If there is anyone that needs counseling, put your name on this sticky note and I will give it to the guidance counselor," she said.

That was my cue. Once a month, my teacher would ask students if they needed to see the counselor. She would pass out unevenly cut yellow slips of paper for our name and each and every time, I'd slide the paper under my desk, write down my name, and then look up to see if anyone was looking. I had serious problems, I thought, and I needed help sorting them out. After everyone lined up for recess or lunch, I would quietly walk to the white box, feel for the slit at the top, and slide my paper in.

Anticipating the meeting always put a smile on my face. It was the only time I felt heard. It felt good to be listened to. A couple of days later, my teacher would tell me to go down to the office. It would be just me and Mrs. Taylor. All eyes and ears were on me. She listened to me cry, tell stories about my father, and express my anger towards my mother. She gave me ways to cope with my situation and then I felt better until the next time the teacher passed around the yellow slips. But this day was different.

I waited until the last person left the room, acting like I was trying to find my books, when they were already in my book bag. I scanned the empty room; only broken pencils with half-eaten erasers were left behind on the floor. I scribbled my name down and slipped it into the box.

"You don't have to do that, Khadija," my teacher said. She had such a sweet and compassionate voice. She wore a sweater with a golden retriever on it and always spoke gently to me. She shifted her sandy blonde hair to the side and knelt beside me. "Since you go every week, don't bother putting your name inside. I will be sure to call you when it's time."

She gave me a hug and told me to hurry on to lunch.

After lunch, I waited for her to call me to the counselor's office. I was in P.E. and I hated it. I couldn't play all the games they played because I had a dress on and while the other kids did the fun exercises—the ones that made you giggle from running back and forth from block to block—the teacher would give me substitute exercises—arm windmills. I had the strongest arms in school.

My teacher finally called my name. I dropped my arms and ran to the building. I walked through the principal's office and as always, I felt special.

"Hello, Khadija," the secretary said.

"Khadija! How are you doing?" The principal said. "Are you ready for the Spelling Bee?"

"Yes!" I said, with a smile. I always won the spelling bee.

He followed behind me. He never followed behind me. It was always just me and Mrs. Taylor, but this time, she wasn't there.

I sat down in my usual miniature blue seat while a counselor sat in a much bigger chair in front of me. The principal pulled up a chair and so did two other strange women. One woman crossed her arms, as if she was about to give a good lecture, while the others wore pity on their faces. *Poor little black girl.* I shuffled in my seat a bit.

"I received a slip from you," the counselor said, as if we were the only two in the office.

"Yes."

The blonde-haired lady, dressed in blue slacks that rode her ankles and a white blouse that traveled up to the middle of her neck, scooted her chair closer to mine. She had gotten so close to me that it made me feel uncomfortable, staring me down like an ancient artifact with her deep blue eyes. She grabbed my tiny, caramel-colored hands. I scooted my butt back in an attempt to move my chair, but I only accomplished filling it up with my tiny body.

She leaned in toward me. "What would you like to talk about today?"

"My dad," I said.

The others looked on intently.

"Go on."

"I miss my dad."

"Where does your father live?"

"He lives in Florida. And every summer, I go see him and we have so much fun. He has a wood shop in the back of his house and he makes furniture for people. He sometimes lets me help. I have my own room there and my own dog. Her name is Princess. She's a Doberman and she plays Nintendo with me. She barks at anyone who comes in the house. She loves me. And I can wear whatever I want there."

"Okay," the counselor said. "But what happened last—"

"And guess what?" I continued.

She nodded, as if following my story word for word.

"He has this snake and I feed it mice. I'm scared of it, though. He took me to Universal Studios and I almost got on 'Double Dare,' but I lost Simon Says. I cried, so he took me to the beach."

"That's sweet," she said, glancing up at the principal.

"You must miss him."

"I do. And I want to move with him, but my mother won't let me."

I forced a tear to come out and then looked back at her with the saddest set of eyes. It always worked on white people. *Maybe she can convince my mother to let me live with him.*

"Your mother loves you," she said. She sat up in her chair and gently grabbed my hand. "Don't you think your mother loves you?"

"Yes," I nodded.

"There are some people here who would like to ask you just a couple of questions about your mother and what happened last night. Do you feel up to talking about that?"

Fear spread from the bottom of my toes, through my legs, up my spine and jarred my words. I suddenly felt betrayed.

"Can you tell us what happened last night?" She said.

I looked into her eyes and then at the others. They were locked in. They didn't care how I felt about my real dad. I stayed silent.

"Khadija. It's important you tell us how you feel about last night. What went on?"

I looked up at the laminated poster board stuck between the wall and putty. It read, "Children are the roots of the future. Nurture it." The smell of broken crayons thickened the air as I looked on the desk and saw scattered crayon boxes, markers, and coloring sheets from other disturbed kids.

I thought about how much I loved my mom and my family, and how it would feel weird telling strangers about what happened in my house. My mother didn't like us to utter a word about family issues. They were strangers trying to be friends long enough to get the gossip. I was starting to understand.

I looked down and talked to my fingers as I picked at my nails. "William and my sister was fighting."

"How do you feel about William?"

I closed my eyes and the thought of him came to mind. He was a tall, dark, and muscular man—a marine, firm and serious. But then I remembered when he would stay up all night playing Monopoly with me. He never yelled at me. He talked to me about school and lectured me about boys and he never let me win. He said that in life, I had to work hard to win in life.

I had to earn it or I wouldn't learn. He taught me how to shoot a perfect jump shot and praised me when I got it right. He took us swimming and dunked us in the pool and after we left the gym, he'd take us to the store and buy us a Mountain Dew to "rehydrate" us.

I looked up at the strangers staring at me and shrugged my shoulders. "I like him."

"So, did he hurt your sister? Last night?"

I shrugged my shoulders again.

"What about your mother? Does she hit you?"

Oh, shoot. You're talking about my mother now, I thought, cringing in my chair. *My mother don't play.*

"Has she ever hit you?"

Doesn't every mother hit their children when they are bad? I hit Stephanie, my doll, when she doesn't sit still in her seat. My mother hits me all the time, I thought.

And right before I was going to tell them the truth, I remembered sitting in that very same office just a few months ago.

I had lost so many battles over the years with my mother, but for once, on that day, I felt like I could win the war. I slid through the lunch line, plotting. I had said something smart to my mother that morning while she pulled my hair into a ponytail, and she hit me with the hardest wooden brush I'd ever felt in my life. She hit the bone. It hurt so bad, just one tear rolled down my face. I was mad. All the rubbing in the world couldn't soothe the pain I felt, and she was going to pay.

"What happened to your hand?" The lunch lady had said.

I glanced down at my hand. "My mother."

I poked my lips out like a sad puppy dog and I recall batting my eyes.

"I'll take you to the office," the woman said. "We might need to call the police."

I pulled back. "No! Don't call the police. I lied. It don't hurt. My mother didn't do it."

She pulled me all the way to the office and I had to pee so bad, a sprinkle came out. They called social services, the police, and my mother up to the school. It was a disaster.

I'd never forget the look on my mother's face when they repeated my animated story of what happened. She shook her head so many times and bit so deep into her lip, it turned red.

Needless to say, my mother got a warning and I got a whipping for opening up my mouth. I got another whipping anytime I did anything wrong, and she remembered that day.

"Nope. My mother never hits me." I shrugged my shoulders, feeling like a warrior. I wasn't a pitiful little girl anymore. They weren't about to get me to talking, then leave me in the hands of my mother.

"I can't remember anything. I pinkie promise."

They let me go and I went back to class.

As I rode the bus back home, I wondered if I had done the right thing. *He must not be that bad; my mother loves him and stays with him. Isn't that what Christians do?*

Yeah. Even the pastor told my mother to stay. I remember now. A vow to God is a vow not to be broken, no matter what.

I felt good. I did the right thing.

I wondered if they told my mother how badly I wanted to live with my dad. She hated it when I asked, so maybe they could convince her it would be better for me.

I walked through the front door of my house, scared of the unknown. There were cops there. My mother hugged me. She was on the phone with someone. William was at work and my sister was in some group home and within weeks, everything was back to normal. But I still yearned to be with my father and my mother still refused to let me go. But if my mother didn't instill anything else in me, it was unbelievable will and unstoppable faith. I would find a way.

Chapter Five

The grass is not always greener on the other side. That is what my mother told me when I wanted to do the dance "the butterfly" like the kids at school, wear boxed braids like Janet Jackson on Poetic Justice, or like my stepmother, whose long micros made her look like an exotic Jamaican Queen.

And by the time my twelfth birthday came around, I was strictly forbidden to mention living with my father because the grass was not always greener on the other side. But it looked pretty Kush to me.

I spent every summer with my father. I was his sidekick, his only child, and he always made me feel like I was the only one in his world. He took me to the beach, where I witnessed my first shooting star and of course, I only had one wish. As the deep blue sky lit up, I wished it would shoot back to North Carolina, tap my mother in the head like a magic wand, and change her mind about me being with my father.

My father would make fun bets with me, saying, "Khadija. I bet you can't eat all seven of those tacos."

"Yes, I can," I said.

"All right. You eat them, but if you throw up on my floor, you're disqualified. If you can hold it in, I'll give you five dollars." He then chuckled at my determination to win.

I sat at the table and stuffed my face until it hurt to breathe. I glanced down at the carpet, swallowed deeply, and took a sip of water. When it was all down, I felt like a proud blowfish.

"I won!"

He slapped a five-dollar bill in my hand.

"If you are the first to buckle up your seatbelt in the car, I will give you ten dollars."

"Ten dollars!"

My eyes lit up like I had won the lottery. I whined. I exaggerated the pain, bent over like someone had shot me in the gut, and when he walked me to the bathroom, I moaned louder until he shut the door.

In my mind, I won the bet, but thirty minutes later, the bathroom spoke volumes to who was really victorious: the tacos. It didn't matter to me, though. An upset stomach gave me a free pass to jump in between my dad and stepmother as they tried to cuddle at night. I'd continue holding my stomach and nestle under my father like a newborn cub.

I watched him grind at his regular job, then work all night on handcrafted tables, desks, and bed sets. He became a salesman, carrying a photo album of his portfolio everywhere we went. He'd walk into city hall, build a desk, and before I knew it, everyone in the precinct knew our names. We never set foot in a church except on Easter or when someone died, but my father had faith. It was a different kind of faith. He believed in himself more than anyone I knew. He made things happen. He was my hero. But even he couldn't talk my mother into letting me live with him.

As thick, curly hairs grew between my legs and I grew taller than my mother, so did my courage. I would wait until the perfect moment, when she wasn't prepared, and I would strike. The perfect moment was Christmas.

While everyone watched their parents pile gift-wrapped Nintendos and Sega Genesis consoles under the Christmas tree, my mother and stepfather piled us all into our station wagon for a road trip to Cleveland.

It was something we did often. My mother was also a daddy's girl and she missed her family a lot. She was one of the youngest out of thirteen kids and when we'd come to visit, we'd walk in smelling the Whiting fish frying on the stove, cornbread rising in the oven, greens simmering in turkey neck juice, and the entire family would greet us with B.B. King playing in the background.

"Dad. Can you come get me?" I begged.

It didn't matter to me how good the food was or who was at my grandmother's house, I was anxious to see my father.

He'd just moved back from Florida to Cleveland after the death of my grandfather. He moved in with my grandmother and uncle, so coming to Cleveland with my mother was a special treat.

"I'll be there in a minute," he said.

A minute was such an understatement. It took hours for him to pick me up from the East Side. While waiting, I'd spend time with my mother's side of the family. Boy, did they know how to have fun. It was the only time I could experience a real house party. They played Bone Thugs N Harmony, Case, Usher, Destiny's Child, and my mother wouldn't say a word, and if she did, my grandfather, with his shiny Jheri curl, would take up for me. As long as I scratched his scalp, he was happy.

He was a gangsta chilling at his leather bar with a glass of Crown Royal in one hand and a Marlboro cigarette in the other. I'd heard he was a beast, too. He didn't play when it came to his daughters. Urban legend had it that he'd found out my mother got hit by her boyfriend. He called the boyfriend over to the house, not hinting he knew a thing. Before you knew it, he'd tied the man to the fire extinguisher and beat him with the butt of his gun, threatening to kill him if he laid another finger on her. He was also my superhero.

There were plenty of kids to play with, but I always seemed to bum a quarter or two and walk with my uncle to the corner store. Cleveland was much different than Jacksonville with its cutthroat streets, but there was one thing they had in common. I was still the strange one.

I was still the girl who couldn't dance worth a lick because in North Carolina, if I thought about bending for anything other than to pick something up, I'd get whipped. I was lighter than everyone else in my family, so I was called "white girl."

"Why you talk like that?" They asked.

When we would play Monopoly and I'd get mad about going to jail, I'd say, "Oh my gosh, that sucks," and when they would go to jail, they would say, "Damn, I'm salty," and I'd look at them as if they were going to hell and they'd look at me as if I thought I was better than them.

"Talk like what?" I asked.

"White."

I shrugged my shoulders. I didn't have a voice and I knew it. They could talk to their mothers about anything, yet at nine years old, I bled through my panties and scraps of toilet paper for days before asking my mother for a pad. I was too afraid to ask her why I was bleeding down there. At twelve years old, I stole my first kiss in the back of the church during benediction and for weeks, I studied the growth of my stomach because I thought I might be pregnant. "Lord!" I begged. "Please don't let me be pregnant. I promise not to ever kiss a boy again!"

He had mercy on me. When I told a friend at school what happened and how God had mercy on me, she just laughed. *You have to have sex, duh.* It only made me feel like an alien in a world full of humans who seemed birthed with social intellect.

The only place I felt like myself was when I was with my father. So, when he picked me up, I was always happy and when he dropped me off, I'd sit in my grandmother's room and cry. Whatever gift he left me with, from a Walkman to a stuffed animal orca from Sea World, I slept with it and carried it everywhere I went. I often fantasized about living with him until it drove me crazy. This particular visit, it did. I lost my ten-year-old mind.

"Please, Ma. Can I move with my father? I promise I won't ask for anything else in my life. He has money, Mom, and he can take care of me. I would have my own room and—"

She was unusually still. It was actually terrifying. "The grass is not always greener on the other side," she said calmly.

"But, Ma. He said I can go to private school and—"

My mother gave me this look. It was an unholy look. She was mad and I didn't understand why. All I wanted was to live with my father.

"But, Ma! I hate living with you."

She lunged across the room with a belt already in her hand. I had no idea where it came from. "Come here!" She yelled.

"No!"

I thought that if I yelled loud enough, my family would come marching up to rescue me, but they didn't.

My world stopped. Suddenly, jumping out the window to get away from her didn't seem like too much of a bad idea. I panicked. I was in my uncle's room, not at home, where I knew the perfect places to dip, dodge, and hide.

She caught me with the belt, straight across my butt. *Dang, Ma. You got good aim all of a sudden.*

I took it like a champ. I had rage, too. And I was sure going to use it—to run.

I spun around her and charged down the steps, but the belt caught my leg. It stung like crazy, but I kept moving. In my mind, I was running away. I would make it down the steps, disappear through the front door, and run as fast as I could from one side of the city to the other. *Who cares about the drug dealers on the corner?* I made it halfway down the steps when I saw the Hulk standing there—my stepfather. He held the wooden banister, blocking my path, messing up my vision. He had this look on his face. He felt sorry for me, but he still wasn't letting me go. I ran back up and there my mother was, standing there with the belt, one hand on her hip, with fire in her eyes.

"What did I tell you?" she said. "You're not living with your father."

"I hate you!" I yelled.

I'm sure every neighbor on the street heard me. And I'm sure they heard the belt, too. She whipped the demons out of me. But still, I wasn't giving up.

I took the whipping, got the whipping hiccups under control, and waited for her to go back downstairs. As soon as it got quiet, I tiptoed my butt to my grandmother's room and called my father.

It rang once. It rang twice and in between, it seemed like an eternity.

"What you doing on the phone?" My grandmother questioned.

My heart dropped and suddenly, I had to boo-boo.

"Hello. Hello." I could hear my father getting louder and louder.

I slid the phone back on the hook. "Nothing," I said.

I eased my way back into my uncle's room and listened as the phone rang downstairs. It was my father. I heard him asking my mother why I had called.

I got a couple of more whacks that night, thinking if I cried and begged hard enough, she'd break. It only made her madder. Eventually, I fell asleep, but I was determined. I would live with my father. Not only did I have faith the size of a mustard seed, but I also had picked up on this special determination and belief in myself from my father. Nothing was going to stop me.

CHAPTER SIX

I couldn't understand for the life of me why my mother wanted me so bad. I'd done everything I could possibly do to be a bad kid. I rolled my eyes when I wasn't in arms reach, I talked to boys on the phone, bumped Tupac when she was at church, and my mood swings got me smacked in my mouth more than I wished. I didn't understand.

"Ma," I said, peeling at my nails.

It was almost midnight and we were driving from church. Seemed like the perfect time to ask, since she'd just finished shouting up and down the aisle of the holy church.

"Mom. Mother. Mother dearest." I smiled through my nerves. "Can I ask you a question?"

She turned down the music. "Sure. Go ahead."

"Um. Why don't you let me live with my dad?"

I'd got it out! I cheered for myself on the inside. I finally asked her the question burning in my mind.

She fell silent. She tapped her fingers against the steering wheel and then glanced back at me.

"Because I love you. Because I want to protect you and I don't want to see you hurt. If only you knew, Khadija. If only you knew." She shook her head, as if she had something heavy on her mind. She'd been through a lot; I'd imagined and often wondered if she was running from something in Cleveland, if something was haunting her there.

She left when I was just two years old. She married my stepfather, a Sergeant in the Marines, and moved to Jacksonville, North Carolina. But something was strange about it all. When I thumbed through her old photo album, she looked free and happy. Her wedding, which seemed fit for a Queen was set in a historic church cathedral. She wore a beautiful white gown which stretched halfway down the center aisle and the church was full of friends and family. It seemed she lived in a different world back then. It was the most beautiful wedding I'd ever seen. But now, we were broke. I didn't understand it.

My mother reached back and patted me on my knee. It was a simple touch, but it meant the world to me.

"I love my children and will do anything for them. That includes you, Khadija."

I was the middle child and always felt like she didn't love me as much as everyone else. She worried herself sick about my oldest sister; my brother's father passed away, so she protected him like no other, and my little brother and sister were so young, they needed her every attention. And then there was me. I didn't even have a godmother.

I had all the rebuttals in the world spinning in my mind, but I nodded in peace. For the first time, I sat still enough to listen. Maybe she wasn't trying to be mean or evil, but she was truly fighting for me. She was protecting me from something.

We arrived home that night and I was anxious to get out of my church clothes. So was my mother. She kicked her shoes off at the door, throwing her choir robe into her room, my siblings and I raced to smash the most roaches before they scurried back into their homes: the dark crevices of the walls, underneath the sink, pots and pans, and even inside the refrigerator door.

My mother turned the stovetop on and started frying gizzards. It was our after church ritual. Ever since I could remember, I ate gizzards, chewed on them until my jaws hurt and snuck into the kitchen when my mother wasn't looking. But one day, while bragging that I loved gizzards, "a friend" told me the truth.

"Ew!" She said as I bragged about the country's best-kept secret. "You eat chicken hearts, livers, and brains. You nasty."

I could have thrown up right there. *No wonder they were chewy*, I thought.

The gizzards were frying in one pot and my mother spooned a thick lump of Crisco into another for the fries.

The grease had gotten hot fast, but still, she threw the fries in like a pro. I stood far away, watching from the living room.

"Get me another bag out the fridge," my mother said.

I sighed to myself. She knew I was scared of the grease.

"Hurry up now, before it start popping." She'd pinch me on my side.

"Ma," I whined.

"Girl. Hurry up, then go put a movie on."

I threw the fries in from fifty feet, still got bit by the grease monster, and went back into the living room to scour for a movie. We had every VHS ever made. From *The Making of Thriller* to *Pretty Woman*.

I listened to my mother hum. She fished for scattered fries and focused on nabbing the floating gizzards. She was in deep thought.

"Ma," I said, walking back into the kitchen. "Do you need any help?"

Her eyes grew big with shock, then she eased into a smile. "No, sweetheart. Thank you."

She dipped her hand back into the bag and grabbed a handful of fries. The mountain of fries had grown much larger than ever before. It took two big plates with napkins at the bottom to soak up the grease. I got excited. I believed the extra fries were for me.

"What are we watching tonight?" She asked.

"It's a surprise!"

"Okay," she said, sprinkling salt on the gizzards and fries.

We watched the same movies over and over again until I knew most of the words.

"No matter how hard it gets. We haven't finished yet. There so much life ahead. We got so much to do..." I'd sing as I popped in *The Five Heart Beats*.

"Nights like this. I wish. Rain drops would fall hall hall hallllll!" And I'd fall down to the floor like Eddie Cain, the crackhead.

It was those classics that brought me hope. It was the life of Tina Turner that reminded me just how powerful a woman with a made-up mind was, and I'd wished with all my heart that my mother knew her own strength. I wanted her to say "no" when she wanted to say no. I wanted her to find her own happiness. It took a whole entire hour of beatings for Tina to realize who she was. I wondered how long it would take my mother.

We chilled together with a mouthful of shoestring fries, a twenty-five-cent pop, and followed the stories, as if we had never seen them before.

Why Do Fools Fall in Love with Frankie Lymon was one of my favorites. He had a certain spark in his eyes every time he got on that stage. It was one I could never forget. He had such passion for what he did, dancing and singing as if his life depended on it. I wanted to be like him. Well, kind of. The scene where he dropped Elizabeth's dog out the window sealed the deal for me. Drugs were bad and would ruin your life. However, his life taught me that life was what you made it. No one escaped it without getting bruised and hurt along the way. The lesson was that we all could really control our destiny, if we worked hard. And in my head, if I worked hard to become an actor or singer, I was sure to get rich. It would be nothing to buy my mother a house.

I couldn't wait to talk to my dad. He usually gave me anything I wanted.

"Dad. If I move with you, can you put me in acting classes?"

"Yeah, Peanut. You can do whatever you want in life. You gotta stick with it, though."

His words were so powerful to me.

As my mother fell asleep on the movie like she always did, I got up and kissed her. Being an emotional teen, I started to understand how difficult it must be for a mother—just a little. Maybe I was too hard on her. Just maybe, it was best to stay with her to make sure she was okay. She was teaching me how to be a good person.

I'd complain every week when she dragged us to an elder's home. She'd plait their hair, laugh, and talk to them, and it made them happy. I, on the other hand, pouted the whole time. "Why do I have to sweep the floors, take out the trash, and wash the dishes? This ain't my house."

"You better honor your elders," she'd say. "You never know when you are going to need a helping hand."

I admired my mother as she slept. It would be the first time I learned to take snapshots of moments I never wanted to forget.

"I love you, too," she said. She sat up just enough to kiss me back.

I went to bed that night thinking about all I could do, even with just a little money, to make her happy. She cared about me and she finally showed it. Rather, that night, I learned that I finally appreciated it. But it wouldn't take long before things changed again. My mother, she would make the ultimate sacrifice, the moment she'd prove just how much she loved me.

CHAPTER SEVEN

This particular night, my mother paced frantically around the house. She was nervous and late for church, talking fast and appearing flustered.

It was hard for me to conceal the joy I felt because I didn't have to go to church.

"You better not cook while I'm gone. And Khadija, don't forget to do the dishes," she said.

She was dressed in a long, navy blue suit with matching sheer stockings and shoes with thick, stubby heels. Her hair was rolled tightly in a bun and she smelled like a blend of warm vanilla and strawberries. I followed her every move, amazed at how fast she and her brain worked.

"Don't forget to wash the dishes and sweep the floor," my mother reminded me. She pondered for a second, trying to figure out what she was forgetting.

"Yeah, do the dishes and then you can play the game."

I was so happy to hear that; I couldn't wait for her to leave. Duck Hunt was calling me, and so was Street Fighter.

All I have to do is the dishes, and on top of that, I don't have to go to church. Cool. I can handle that, I thought.

"Oh, and no cooking," she blurted while running out of the house.

When we finally heard the door slam, my brother and I did the moonwalk halfway across the room. I turned on the radio, hoping they'd play my favorite song within the next hour—"Waterfalls"— and my brother channeled the TV to play the Nintendo.

We had exactly fifteen minutes. If she didn't come bursting through the door within that time, we knew she was at church, in the choir stand, singing to the Lord.

As soon as it felt safe, we jumped on. No need to worry about the dishes. It would take her at least two hours to come back home.

It was my turn and my brother was itching for me to get burned by fireballs or split open by the ninja's flying axes. We were both sitting on the floor Indian-style. We were so close to the 13-inch boxed TV, we could have kissed Luigi himself. It was our version of a house party. Especially since we could turn the volume up the loudest and be completely zoned out—absolutely no interruptions. It was all fun and games, until we heard a key slide into the doorknob.

I jumped up in shock, but was not quick enough. The door had opened and my stepfather, John, appeared. The look on my face screamed I was guilty and awaiting sentencing.

He stared back at me. It was an intense and intimidating stare, one I'd always feared. I looked away. It was much easier to just focus on the game.

"Why are you playing the game? Didn't your mother tell you to do the dishes?"

My heart beat just a little bit faster, but still, I was too afraid to look up at him. I shrugged my shoulders instead.

"Mom said," I stuttered. My hands began to shake, my voice quivering over each syllable. "Mom said to wait until she get back because we don't have enough dishwashing liquid."

I don't know where that lie came from, but it seemed to work. A slight conniving grin formed on my face. I don't know where that came from, either.

He eyed me for a second, taking in every word, examining the wavelengths of my voice. He was a Marine. He possessed the discipline of a Marine and commanded respect, but this time, he walked away.

My heart pounded so hard, I wanted to grab my chest, but I concealed it by jerking my hands on the remote controller up, down, and around to the movements of Mario. The further he moved away from us, the calmer I became, and the moment he shut his bedroom door, I knew I had won.

A couple of hours passed and my mother finally made it home. Walking in on us playing the game made her furious—an "I can't take it anymore" kind of madness. It's something about video games that made her and all the adults I knew fly off the hinges. I had always thought it was jealousy that we were free to play and not working. It was something about the noise, the excitement, and the freedom we had that sparked something crazy within them. At least, that is what my imagination told me.

She wrestled with her words. I guess she was trying to say too much too fast. I couldn't understand a word.

"Did you do them dishes like I told you?"

My eyes said it all. *It wasn't that I didn't want to do them. I just got caught up in the game*, I thought. I wanted to say it, but instead, I dropped my head.

"Come here," she snapped.

I got up and met her at the back of the couch, facing her about an inch away from arm's-length, just in case she got the urge to swing.

Almost at the same time, I heard the door open in the back room. Those heavy footsteps getting closer and closer to me meant trouble. *Dang-gone it,* the little in my voice whispered. *This can't be good.*

He didn't even get out of the hallway good enough before he started fussing. "Khadija, I thought you told me that you were not supposed to do the dishes today?"

Once again, those piercing eyes put fear and hesitation in me. I couldn't think. The world was moving too fast.

"What?" I replied. I rolled my eyes and smacked my lips.

He looked at me and his eyes bulged with fury. "What you say?"

His words were like a bullet ricocheting throughout my body, sending straight fear through my veins.

My words jumbled, "I said, my motha—"

He snatched my neck so fast, I lost my breath.

"WILLIAM ... NO!" my mother screamed.

He pushed my body against the spine of the couch, his hand wrapped around my neck.

My mother pushed her body weight against his, yelling and screaming and trying to free me.

I looked him in his dark brown eyes, scared senseless.

Was he going to punch me, throw me across the room or was he going to let me go? Please let me go.

"Who do you think you're talking to?" he yelled.

My mother grabbed his arms, but the muscles were too massive to get a good grip. Like a rag doll, he shoved her into the glass table with his free hand. She fell to the floor. "WILLIAM!" she screamed again.

"You better not never talk to me like that again," he said. He let go of me after threatening my soul and slowly walked back into his room. I patted down my neck to make sure it was still there and intact and then I ran to the phone. I was calling 911. He wasn't getting away with this one.

"Khadija!" My mother called. "Put the phone down, now! We are Christians!" she yelled, fighting back tears.

I watched her as she pulled herself up from the floor. I put the phone down.

She disappeared into the hallway, double-stepping to her bedroom; I guess to smooth things over with my stepfather. I had other plans. In my mind, this was the perfect opportunity to get out of this house for good, and I was sure going to use it. I picked up the phone again, dialed the 216 number, and went to town. Tears falling and voice trembling, I set the stage. "Dad, he hit me!"

Those three words changed my life. While I was spilling the beans, my mother walked in, looking discombobulated. But the beans were already out, all over the floor, and she was too late to clean them up.

She grabbed the phone. "What are you doing?"

"I called my dad."

She looked at me with such pain in her eyes, I wanted to cry. I wanted to take it back. I had double-crossed her, backstabbed her—her very own daughter. She hated for anyone to know about anything that was going on in our house, especially my dad.

"Mom, he can beat on you, but he sure not going to beat on me."

I slapped myself in the mouth. I couldn't believe what I had just said, or the way it came out with such passion and strength. I never talked to my mother in that manner before, but I was talking out of pure desperation. I hated wearing dresses every day, I hated being different everywhere I went, and I hated living under my mother's strict rules. I needed to be free.

My mother got on the phone, begging for my father to calm down. I watched the tears flow down her beautiful face as she tried concealing her shame. Her strong and relentless soul had broken and it was me who shattered her world.

Before the night was over, she told me to start packing my bags because I had finally got what I wanted. My dad was picking me up in two days and I was moving to Cleveland. That was the sweetest news I had ever heard.

As I packed my bags, I admired my room for the first and last time. Suddenly, the little things my mother had done to make the room look good stood out to me. The decor came mostly from the thrift store, but they were bought out of love.

"Why are you packing?" My little sister said, as she held onto the dolls we both played with.

"I gotta go," I said. I wouldn't look her in her eyes.

She stared at me as if I'd torn her world apart. "But why? Why can't you just stay here?"

I stuffed my book bag in silence. All the years I wanted to leave, I never thought I would hurt those I left behind—my brother and sister. I couldn't believe I was missing my room already and my church family and the many trips to the basketball court with my stepfather. It was kind of cool to go swimming on the military base on hot summer days and when he'd come home from serving the country, he'd watch wrestling with us. He'd sit by the closet, spray-starch his uniform stiff and then shine his boots so well I could see my very own reflection in them. And then the glow-sticks. Those were the best. He'd snap them in half and light up the entire room, then he'd hand them to us. He'd take us to the USO and we'd play arcade games.

I couldn't believe I was leaving my family.

Those thoughts didn't last long as I heard my mother talking to my father the next day. That's when reality hit my thirteen-year-old conscience. *Was I making the right decision. Was Cleveland as cool as I thought? Was the grass greener on the other side or did the bright, shining sun alter my perspective?*

My father arrived. I watched him pull up in the parking lot from my mother's bedroom and got excited. He talked to my mother in our living room and I wanted him to stay just a little longer, but he said we had to get back on the road. I just wanted to spend a little more time with my mother. *When would be the next time I could see her?*

She walked us out to the car and I lived in that moment for as long as I could. "Keep her in the church," she said. "Don't forget; you promised me she would stay in the church."

My mother embraced me like never before. She kissed me on the cheek. "I love you, Dee."

She stood there by the curb, watching as my father pulled off, then she turned around. But I kept watching her. I fought back the tears because I really did love my mother and I wanted her to know it. I fought back the pain of a child leaving her mother because I had too much pride to give her one last real hug. I didn't even realize how much I'd missed her until I watched her drop her head down and slowly disappear into the hallway to our apartment.

I imagined her going straight to her room and falling down to her knees in prayer. Prayer that God was going to cover me and make sure I didn't stray from Him, prayer that I would forever be covered in His blood. But little did she know, I had a prayer of my own.

As I caught the last glimpse of my mother, I closed my eyes and I made a promise to her. I would come back for her. I would work my butt off in Cleveland, get the best grades, and go to college. I would come back, buy her a house, and she would never have to worry about money again. She could live the life she always dreamed of. My promise to her made me feel better. It gave me unimaginable drive.

Bye, Mom.

PART TWO

In North Carolina, the sun shined during the winter months, but in Cleveland, the clouds sagged from the sky, the bitter air slapped you in the face for having the nerve to walk outside, and cars bustled in the street with a foot of snow on the ground. This city was 'bout it, 'bout it, and this Southern girl was ready. School started in just two days.

Kirk Middle School reminded me of an old cathedral, a palace built back in the early 1900s. The tainted paint from the tall ceilings peeled back from the wall, black mold grew infectious as students opened their fifty-year-old math books, and the harsh yellow lights made the place seem dreary. Yet, there were athletic trophies displayed in antique glass cases and club sign-up sheets taped to the wall. There were black, brown, and light-skinned students walking with their heads held high, with sharp, confident attitudes, wearing clothes from Macy's and hairstyles straight out of *Black Hair Magazine*.

Then there was me.

I walked in class with cornrows tighter than Queen Latifah in the movie *Set It Off*. I rocked my stepmother's Eighties hammer pants and had a limp that matched my thug. I wasn't going to be intimidated at this school. I made sure I was cool on my first day of school; besides, I was wearing pants.

I closed the door behind me and faced the class head-on. They were black. Every last student sitting in the class looked like me.

"Here," I said to the teacher.

I tossed my hall pass onto her desk and scanned the room for an empty seat.

No one said a word to me. I returned the favor.

"Class," Mrs. Stewart said.

The teacher was a thick woman with a big voice. Her box braids thinned her edges, but the braids themselves were on point. With just one word, everyone went silent.

"Your assignment for the weekend is to take the lyrics to a song and then break down the meaning. Monday, you will each share it with the class."

WHAT! I couldn't believe my luck. *Shoot!*

The whole hour, I couldn't consume a word of what she was teaching. All I could think about was how they would judge me like the other black kids did. Call me "white girl" for speaking proper, tell me I didn't act black enough and that I must have been from Europe, not Africa, because I was much too light. North Carolina all over again.

The bell rang and already, I was ready to go home. I worked my finger along my schedule, squinting at the room numbers, and that's when he walked up to me.

"What's up?" He said. "I'm Derrick."

He put his hand out like a gentlemen, but all I could do was stare at him.

Derrick was just an inch shorter than my 5'6"; he wore a sharp fade, a huge Kool-Aid smile, and three slits in his eyebrows like Kris Kross.

"What's up?" He said, as I continued to stare. "You okay?"

I giggled, covering my smile. "Yes."

I'd never really been around boys like that. Rather, they never cared to speak to Ms. Holy Poly. This was foreign.

"I'll walk with you to class," he said.

"Okay."

Love was in the air. I couldn't stop cheesing. Silly butterflies fluttered around my tummy and I couldn't control the thrill in my voice. I'd planned our wedding and honeymoon destination before we even made it to the next class.

He walked close to me, head nodding at his boys, giving them some kind of O.G. grip. He looked so proud to have me by his side, introducing me to everyone.

"What are they doing over there?" I asked my new boyfriend.

"Them right there? Oh. She like it," he said.

My jaw dropped, looking at the two, a boy and a girl hiding in a corner. The boy massaged the girl's breasts like Sunday morning biscuits and it seemed normal to everyone but me.

I longed to pull her to the side and tell her that Jesus loved her, witness to her like we did in North Carolina to save our neighbors from burning in hell. But when she cut her eyes at me, I decided it was none of my business. She could do what she wanted.

After school, I clutched my books deep against my chest, forgetting I had a thugged-out limp and hardcore demeanor, and waited for my neighbor to walk home with me. What I really wanted was to see Derrick before I left. Maybe he could walk me home. I stood there on the steps, taking in my new, life accompanied by the aroma of weed and Black and Milds. I'd learned so much from Derrick and I would soon learn much more. He said he would teach me much, much more.

Cars rushed by, men opened their car doors while still rolling down the street, bumping Master P and Tupac's "I Ain't Mad at Cha," and everyone seemed to vibe together. It wasn't as divided as it had been in Jacksonville. There was a sense of community. Even the security guard rocked to the music as he gave fists and grips to students while ushering them off campus. People were free to be themselves in Cleveland. They could talk, dress, and listen to whatever they wanted. I wanted that freedom. I had been waiting for it all my life.

I couldn't wait to get home to tell someone about my day. My father was at work, and so was my stepmother and grandmother, but my uncle was in the attic and that made me happy.

"Uncle Trey!"

"Hey, Niece," he said. "How was your first day of school?"

"It was a'ight," I said, mimicking the slang of my new peers.

He laughed.

I stood there watching him work his fingers on his music mastering board. He had a full studio up there. He mixed and mastered music, was a teacher during the day, and played in a band on nights and weekends.

I plopped down on his futon and tore through my book bag. "I have to explain the meaning of a song and present it in front of the entire class."

"You got it," he said. "You scared?"

"Yesss."

"All right, then. What song you thinking about?"

"I don't know. I was thinking 'Silver and Gold' by Kirk Franklin or 'This is the Day the Lord Has Made'."

He laughed. "Is that the song you would pick or the song your mother would pick?"

I shrugged my shoulders. "I don't know."

"Stand up!" he said.

I stood up.

"Stand up tall and proud and tell me what song *you* love." He placed his hand on my heart. "Look at me. Right here," he said, pointing to his eyes.

"Who are you?" he said.

"I don't know," I said, turning away.

"Look at me, Khadija Barnes. Who are you?"

"I don't know!" I yelled.

I looked into his hazel eyes and wanted to cry. It seemed like all the other girls at school were brave. They knew what they wanted to wear, and they were confident to speak up, but me, I was told what to do, what not to do, how think, and what to say. Anything else, and I'd get a whipping.

"You're going to have to find yourself."

"I don't know what you mean." I threw myself down onto his futon and buried my face in the cushion. "No matter where I go, I am always the outcast. I can't fit in anywhere."

"You're not supposed to. No one person is just like any other. We are all very different, with different tastes and different ideas. It's up to you to be brave enough to embrace what makes you different."

He handed me a book. "First, you have to start reading. Now, Khadija, what is your favorite song?

My weary eyes met his. "I like Tupac."

"Why?" he said, walking around me as if he were my teacher.

The words *I don't know* were on the tip of my tongue, but his eyes begged for the truth.

I thought about it. "Well. I like 'Brenda's Got a Baby' because it's a story and I like stories. And I love 'Dear Momma,' too. I guess because it's a story."

"Good. Now say it with confidence."

"But I can't, Uncle Trey. They don't like me there. They are going to say I talk too white or something."

"Have they said that yet?"

"No."

"Y'all are all the same. Unique, but you come from the same roots. You will be okay. Now, let me get back to work. Come back and I'll help you with the rest."

"Thanks!"

"No problem."

I walked down to the kitchen. My grandmother was kneading dough and slapping the excess flour from her hands. My father was looking for something in the dining room and although I had a baby brother, a brother one year younger than me and a sister, I felt like the chosen one. I was the special one and nothing could ever change that.

"Do you want to help me bake a sweet potato pie?" My grandmother asked.

"No, thank you," I said.

"Do you want to go to church with me tonight?"

I glanced up at my father, then I thought about what my uncle said. I had to start making my own decisions.

"No." I said. "I want to stay here." I waited for her answer, for her to condemn me, but she didn't. She said, "Okay," and that was the end of it.

My uncle was right. It felt good standing up for what I wanted for a change.

CHAPTER NINE

Monday morning came and I'd worried myself sick. I sat in the back row, hoping the teacher would forget she had a new student, while everyone else was anxious to share.

"Class," Mrs. Stewart said. "Close your mouths. We don't have a lot of time. Khadija. You're first."

My stomach dropped. I eyed her, wishing she could see the fear in my eyes, hoping she would call on somebody else. She was picking on me, I concluded. She didn't like me because I was light-skinned.

I smacked my lips, then caught myself. The fear that my mother would jump from any desk at anytime and slap the rebellion out of me still ran through my veins.

I looked around at the twenty or so kids sitting amongst me and wondered why I was the lucky one to go first. I shuffled my notecards, took a deep breath, and walked up to the front of the class.

"Look at her floods! She drowning!" a girl yelled.

The laughter jarred me, hitting the back of my spine.

"Shut up," Derrick said. "Leave my girlfriend alone."

I looked down at what she was pointing at and couldn't understand what was so funny about my pants. There were new pants this time; I'd gotten them from Kmart. I thought I had gotten it right. I glanced down at how everyone else was wearing their pants and then looked back at mine. They were shorter, yes. I looked a little closer. Oh, they were *much* shorter and my white crew socks boasted their ripples as if they were an accessory.

I sighed, shaking my head. *At least I have a boyfriend*, I thought.

I battled the anxiety consuming my thoughts. And then I remembered what my uncle said: *"Khadija. Be yourself and don't give a damn how anyone else feels about it. They will respect you more if you just get up there and be yourself."*

I lifted my head high despite the laughter and the shushing of my teacher.

"My song is 'Keep Ya Head Up' by Tupac. The reason I chose this song is because Tupac was a storyteller."

The class grew quiet. Only the sporadic whining of the old water heaters could be heard.

"Tupac used lyrics to inspire us, to make us think, stories that helped us relate. He is my inspiration. No matter how tough things get, he said, 'Things will get easier.' But he didn't just *say* it, he came from a mother who was a Black Panther and so he wanted every listener to believe it."

I looked down at the floor and my floods. "That's it."

There was silence and my nerves toiled deep in my stomach.

"Did you bring something for us to listen to?"

"Yes, Ma'am."

I pulled out my CD player, placed it inside the box, and watched as the kids came alive. They rocked to the beat, they proudly sang the song, and they nodded as if they understood.

I remember Marvin Gaye used to sing to me. He had me feelin' like Black was the thing to be.

I closed my eyes while mouthing his truths. It stripped every ounce of fear from my body and it loosened me up.

And I realize Momma really paid the price, she nearly gave her life to raise me right.

I opened my eyes. That was the first time I'd heard that verse like that. It stuck to me this time - made me miss my mom.

"In conclusion," I said. "I'm from a military town called Jacksonville, North Carolina, where there is a lot of white people."

The students whispered; their eyes bucked as they scratched their heads. They held onto my every word.

"And I wanted to live like white people because I thought only white people was rich. I thought that if I was white, I wouldn't have to be poor and I wouldn't have to live in bad neighborhoods. But now that I am here, I learned from my very cool uncle that I can be whoever I want to be. I am black, and I should be very proud. The color of my skin won't stop me unless I let it and I think that is what Tupac was saying."

They clapped. They roared louder than I'd ever heard from anyone my age. I smiled so big on the inside, it lifted my heart. I was part of a community now - a community that understood me. And as I looked into their eyes, and at the teacher who vibed the whole time, I realized I was just like them and they were just like me.

They were black and beautiful. And although, I knew they walked by the same boarded-up buildings, passing homes painted red, claiming it's Blood territory, with doped-up crackheads as neighbors, they carried a sense of pride.

I began to feel that pride. It was powerful. Resilience.

After class, my boyfriend, my sweetheart, came to my rescue.

"Don't worry. You still cute," he said.

I smiled. No boy had ever looked at me the way he looked at me. At lunch, he sat by me, even offering me his tater tots. I scooped them off his tray and started gobbling them down.

"So," he whispered. He scooted so close to me, I could smell the milk on his breath.

"You wanna have sex? We been together for three days now."

"What?" I said. "You crazy?"

I couldn't believe what I heard. My mind must have been playing tricks on me.

"I'm just playing," he said, forcing a smile.

I snatched his tater tots off my plate and plopped them onto his tray. I got up and walked to another table.

It was the first time I stood up to a boy and it felt good. I said, "No." I walked away with my head held high. I was beginning to see my worth and my uncle often reminded me who I was becoming.

The rest of the school year was easy. It didn't matter if I couldn't dress, or how I wore my hair; I finally found a place where I belonged.

By the end of the school year, I was so accustomed to my new life that walking the streets of East Cleveland didn't bother me. Weed wasn't really a drug, I had picked up the new art of cursing, and I excelled at school. However, those were not the only shocking things I'd learn. For the first time, I also witnessed real discrimination.

The suburban school in North Carolina had newer books, brighter rooms, less students, and more teachers who had nothing to worry about but grading papers and breaking up the occasional fight. At my new school, there was great pressure from the state to perform well on standardized tests. School was more like reciting than learning. There was less money and supplies for the arts and the poverty mindset of the students weighed heavy on the teachers. I was starting to see the life Tupac saw when he wrote, "Changes," something I could not understand before.

At home, I was also very happy. My father and I grew closer, but I missed him a lot. I wrote him poetry and he framed it. He took me everywhere with him, even to his job at an automotive store called Auto Zone. I knew every item on the floor and would guide customers according to their needs. We shared a love for music. As soon as the last customer left the floor, he'd crank up the car stereo demo, blasting TLC, Prince, and Roger Troutman, and we'd jam together, laugh together, and eat good. Lunchtime was my favorite with him. I could choose whatever I wanted, from fish dinners to Polish Boys— big, thick sausages topped with fries, coleslaw and barbecue sauce. We broke bread together and talked about everything. He told me his secret crush, Janet Jackson, and I told him mine, Will Smith. Nothing could tear us apart.

Dear Mom,

I told you. The grass is greener on the other side.

CHAPTER TEN

The summer came and like any other teen, I was happy. I spent most of the summer in my uncle's attic, where books on Philosophy consumed most of its space. There was a futon, no bed, as if sleep was insignificant. His passion for music stole its place on the back wall; his guitar, keyboard, mic, and studio equipment took up the rest of the room.

The smoldering heat seemed to rise and suffocate me up there, but I didn't care. It was a place I could be myself, a place where I wasn't judged by my mistakes. Mistakes were encouraged, and the goal was learning who I was.

My uncle was magical and from time to time, he would spread some of his fairy dust on me. He'd give me books to read, take me to the spiritual store, and school me on the meaning of dreams and psychic healing. I never saw him sleep. My father was a businessman, but my uncle was a hustler and he sought to teach me everything he knew.

When we were not in the attic, we were out traveling the country. One of my most memorable trips was to Pennsylvania.

We'd jump into my uncle's white Aerostar caravan with tinted windows and a rainbow streak as a door decal. It was packed with studio equipment. It was just as muggy inside as it was outside. I enjoyed the wind blowing through my hair, my uncle a joint snug between his lips. It took us an hour of trailing through dirt roads and dark, sketchy woods, but soon, we would be safe at my great-grandfather's house.

My great-grandfather, James Lee, was a tall and dark man with the love of God pouring from his every word. He was in his eighties yet carried himself like a warrior. He still had callouses on his hands from building homes over the weekends and walked proudly around his junkyard full of old cars and metal scraps he managed in his backyard. He had a raspy voice and could sing hymns that hummed to your soul.

The first trip, I learned so much about who I was and where my ancestors had come from as I did our second and third trip. But the fourth trip up to the wooded boondocks would be my most memorable.

There were no streetlights going up to Poppa's place. We took our time going up the mountain. I feared wild animals would claw at the car or even worse, zombies would chase us and push us off the cliff to eat us for dinner. My imagination ran wild as we slowly beat the rough path through the woods. However, it was the unusually quiet night that really struck my nerves.

We'd done our job, recording my grandfather's hymns and placing them onto a cassette tape to edit out later. We excused ourselves after dinner and told him we'd be right back. We both jumped in the backseat of the van as we watched my great-grandfather's shadow roam from room to room. He couldn't see us, but we observed his every move. My uncle grabbed his joint from his t-shirt pocket and drew it to his lips.

"Can I hit it?" I asked.

"Naw," he said. "You crazy? Your father would kill me."

I smacked my lips, slouching deeper into the chair and sulked. "Why not?"

"Because, you ain't ready."

I gazed out the window and looked up at the full moon. It looked larger than the tiny planet I lived on.

There weren't any city lights taking away from its beauty, allowing the star to accent the blue sky boldly, sitting on its throne amongst the sparkling stars.

"Please. I can handle it," I said.

I'd watched plenty of my peers do it. It was the norm.

It had only been a week ago that he'd taken me to the Asian Medicine store. I'd sat there in amazement as they cooked up what looked like sticks, stones, and dirty leaves.

"That right there is natural medicine," my uncle had said. "It will heal you faster than any Western pill they can conjure up. Everything you need comes from the earth, even this right here," he said, blowing reefer from his lungs.

"I do recall, Uncle Trey," I said in the van. "You said it was medicine. How can medicine hurt me?"

"All right. All right."

He took a long hit and then passed it to me. My heart raced as I pinched it and set the dry, twisted paper between my lips. I pursed my lips, pulling as much smoke from the joint as I could. I choked. I coughed. It burned a hole through my throat.

"What the fuck? Fuck this shit!" I yelled as I struggled to pull myself up. It was an instant high, my head spinning wildly into the universe.

"Shhh. You too loud," he said, chuckling as if he could barely control himself.

I looked at him and then back at the moon.

"Why the moon moving?" I said. "Is it falling?"

I grabbed my uncle's shoulder. I looked him deep into his eyes. "Oh my gosh. I'm dead!"

I grabbed the door and yanked it open, sticking my head out and screaming, "Get me out of here!"

"Get back in the damn car," my uncle said.

He pulled me back in.

"But I wanna leave. I want to go on a walk," I begged.

He took another long hit, crushed the tip into the ash tray, and threw his head back, allowing the smoke to escape.

"You wanna go, huh?" He opened the door.

"Let's go."

He helped me out of the van.

"Where we going?"

"We're going back in the house."

I stopped, yanking his arm back. "No! But I'm high."

The dizziness caught me off-guard. I could barely stand up. My head hurt, and I had no idea how to control my fast, rotating thoughts. "Am I going to die?" I asked.

"No!" He laughed. He seemed to be having a good ole time while I felt like my spirit was gone from my body. I slapped him on the shoulder and laughed.

We walked back to the house and every step of the way, I grew more and more anxious. *What if my great-grandfather smelled it? What if he told my dad? My dad had never even taken a drink in his life. He would surely be disappointed in me.* I tried not to sway, but my world kept spinning. I fought to think about how I would act if I weren't high, but I couldn't remember that far back.

"Hey. Y'all back," my great-grandfather said. He had such a big smile on his face.

I put my head down, watching my uncle's feet as he walked. I was ashamed.

"Why don't y'all just sit down with me? I want to tell you one more story before I lay down."

My jaw dropped. It felt like I was in the "Twilight Zone." *Really? Out of all the times, he wants us to listen to a story now?*

I pulled up a chair—which took a hell of a lot of concentration to do—and sat down. I smiled at him, staring at him for at least a minute.

"So, let me tell you about the time—"

I sighed in agony. I couldn't stop moving. It felt like I'd just consumed a box of energy drinks and my butt hurt from sitting on the hard, wooden chair. I also had to pee. I looked up at him and smiled again.

Every word that came from his mouth was torturous. I was hungry, sleepy, and growing more irritated by the minute. But soon, he finished.

I ran to the bathroom and was more than happy to do the number two—something I would have felt self-conscious about before—and I hummed to myself.

Then I went into the guest room.

"I need help," I said to my uncle as he passed by my door.

I was still so high, I could barely find the head of the bed. The mound of knitted blankets seemed to be made from straight wool; they were so heavy and thick.

He walked into my dark room and hugged me.

"I'm so high," I said. "I can't sleep."

He laughed under his breath.

"Can you stay with me for a little bit?"

"Yes," he whispered.

CHAPTER ELEVEN

By the time we got back to Cleveland, I wondered if my father could tell I wasn't his little girl anymore. I wasn't interested in childish games. I was a woman now.

It became harder to smile, unless I was with my uncle. I only wanted to spend time with him and I despised anyone getting in the way of that. It was him and me against the world. Loyalty. I stood by it.

Over the rest of the summer, I'd gotten high so much, I'd graduated to picking the sticks, rolling, and even smoking roaches, pipes, and controlling my high around my family.

I couldn't look my father in his eyes. Shame consumed me. I was no longer an innocent little girl running into her father's arms.

Instead, I became the biggest sinner. If I went back to North Carolina, my mother would have rebuked every demonic sin I had committed and drowned me in the name of Jesus. But she wasn't there. And when she called, I feared she would hear the demons rattling in my voice.

"How are things going?" she asked.

"Good," I whispered.

"So," she'd say. "Your sister just made the honor roll."

"That's cool."

"And your brother, well, he can't wait until you come see his basketball games. He made varsity."

"That's cool."

"So, when do you think you'll be coming to visit us?"

"I don't know."

I could hear my little brother and sister in the background talking. They'd stopped asking for me a long time ago. I'd heard that my sister was dealing with some things—bullying, boys, and not feeling pretty enough. They were the same things I had gone through, but I never bothered talking to her about them. I wasn't there. I didn't care.

"So, what have you been up to?" My mother asked.

I rolled my eyes. I mocked her under my breath, wishing I was bold enough to smack my lips and tell her how I really felt. She had so much control over me.

How am I doing? I thought to myself. *Way better than when I lived with you. It's your fault I'm awkward and can't dress and don't know how to do my hair. It's your fault I stick out and boys don't bother to talk to me.*

"Khadija. We miss you."

Yeah, right. All you care about is my relationship with God. What about my relationship with you? What about all the years you missed Field Day because you were busy working? I bet you would have never missed choir practice or the church's anniversary. I can't remember the last time you held me, gave me a simple kiss, or laughed so hard with me, it hurt. You don't love me. You love God more than anything in this world. But that's okay. I've found love.

"A'ight, Ma. I gotta go."

I sighed.

She hung up the phone.

"I can't stand my mother!" I shouted, slamming the phone onto the receiver.

My uncle was walking past the kitchen window when he heard me. "What did you say?"

I peeked out the window.

He shook his head, walking with his guitar case slung across his back, his amp in his hand, its cord draped along his chest.

"Come here, KD."

The neighbor's dogs were barking outside, chasing him back and forth through the driveway.

I stood back from their evil snarls.

"Yes?"

"Don't you ever say that again."

He looked down at me. It had been the first time in a long time that he treated me like my a fourteen-year-old. I must have really pissed him off.

"But I mean it. I hate my mother!" I shouted. "You don't know!"

"No, you don't understand," he said.

The sun bared down on us both, as sweat gathered around my forehead. I was afraid that he, too, would think I was bad. I couldn't lose him, too. I fought the tears back. There was so much going on inside, I could barely control it.

"Did you know almost every single man your mother was with beat her? I'm not talking about a slap here and a slap there. She was punched, she was kicked around, and got told she wasn't shit."

I choked on his bluntness. "No."

"Did you know she probably wanted to get out of Cleveland, so you wouldn't end up like her? She made sacrifices for you and you have the nerve to hate her?"

My knees weakened, every word cutting me down shorter and shorter. "No."

"What I tell you about making assumptions?"

"Ignorant people make assumptions," I mumbled.

"If you know how hard it is, why don't you do something about it? Shut up talking like you know everything, and work hard and change her situation. You focused on the wrong thing. Live a little before you say how easy it is for your mother. It's not easy out here."

"Okay."

"So, is that what you're going to do? Are you going to work hard for your mother?"

"Yes."

"You sound unsure."

"YES!"

"Khadija, there is no greater gift you could give to your mother. I can guarantee you that."

"But how? How am I supposed to make it? I don't even know what I want to go to college for."

He smiled at me. "I'm glad you asked."

He dipped his head into the van window and pulled an orange, glossy book out.

"What is that? A kid's book?" I complained. "I'm reading *Flyy Girl* and *The Coldest Winter Ever*. I ain't no kid anymore."

"It's not a kid's book. It was written by a girl your age. She lived in the projects and she wrote a story about her life and how bad she wanted to make it out. You see those awards she got?" He tapped on the silver pendants etched into the cover. "I bet you they'll pay for her college. If you submit a story and win, they will make it into a book. You should do it. You got skills. This is a great place to start."

"But I write poems. I don't write stories."

"Yeah, but you are a writer. And you're not just *any* writer. You have a gift."

I squinted my eyes against the sun, blocking its rays with my arm.

"I'm not that good at it. I write about hurting people and how people hurt me."

"So, you write your truths. It's hard for people to admit their truths. You keep being real with yourself and you gonna go far. You won't ever have to worry about your mom again. That's a promise. I know you want to help her. I know you miss her."

I shook my head, but he was right. I *did* miss her. And I wanted to help her. And if my uncle said that I could do it, that meant I could. I squeezed him so tight, I didn't want to let go. "Thank you for not giving up on me."

"I gotta go now. You don't want me to be late for my gig, do you?"

"I'm coming with you."

"Nope," he said. "It's at a bar."

"So? You took me to a bar before."

"This different," he said, sliding the van door shut.

"But I can help you carry your things."

"No."

"Please!"

"No."

I stood up tall, mimicking a strong black woman. I cleared my voice. "I promise. I won't tell."

"Promise?"

I smiled. "Promise."

CHAPTER TWELVE

I was introduced as his niece, whenever we'd go anywhere together. He seemed proud to be a father figure and everyone admired that about him. He treated me like a princess, and it seemed as if he was molding me into a future queen. It didn't matter where we went; people loved him, and he could get me into any establishment with just a nod and a smile.

The music in the club mesmerized me. Women were dancing, showing off their curves, while men drooled and howled at them. It cracked me up.

I would make up stories in my head, wondering who the serial killer was and who would become his next victim. I grew up on "Unsolved Mysteries," so the men seemed more like predators, and the women like their prey. I thought it was only a matter of time before a beautiful girl would go missing and end up on the back of a milk carton.

My uncle would get on the stage, pulling me away from my dark imagination. He'd close his eyes and strum his guitar as if he'd traveled to another universe. I admired that. Passion moved people, like Frankie Lymon and Tina Turner. They were able to escape, and I yearned to do the same.

We would get home at around seven or eight o'clock. He'd still be high off music, pure joy exuding from his laughter, beaming from his spirit. I'd turn up the music as if we were on a tour bus, his passion pouring into me. And once we'd get home, we'd sit on the porch and reminisce about the night. I was his loyal and very dedicated student and he was my teacher.

"Once you get you together, I promise you, the right man is going to appreciate the hell out of you. First, you gotta be confident. If you don't learn your worth, you gon' end up with insecure men who can't handle you mentally, so they'll try to handle you physically, like your mom."

I turned down the music and shrugged my shoulders. I fantasized about having a man who treated me like a queen. Opening car doors for me, holding my hand, and laughing at the dumbest things. I imagined myself being a boss and having little boss babies and being happy. I wouldn't have to rely on a man. That was what my mother did and that was her biggest mistake, I assumed. I would do better, I promised myself. All I needed to learn was how to be an amazing woman and everything else would fall into place. At least that is what my uncle told me. I believed every word he said. He never let me down.

And then came Marcy whistling and strolling down the street.

Marcy reminded me of Felicia from the movie *Friday*. She was a bugaboo. A bug I wished I could have squashed and flicked off the porch. She was tiny, short, and was missing her back teeth. She had a walk that was borderline crippled, but she caught her hip and strutted as best as she could.

"What's up, Marcy?" My uncle said.

"Hey, Trey. Hey, Khadija," she'd reply.

I'd turn my nose up at her. She looked raggedy to me. She didn't deserve his attention.

A crackhead? Really? I would think as she stumbled up onto the porch.

Those nights, I saw a different side of my uncle. The way he looked at her with such lust in his eyes; I envied it. It was the same way Brother Ray looked at me. And as she followed him up to his attic, leaving me in the living room to cry and feel lonely, I realized the power of a woman. I wanted to be a woman so bad. I wanted control.

I slid my headphones over my ear and listened to K-Ci & JoJo until anger got the best of me. I grabbed a knife from the kitchen, not knowing what I would do with it, but it gave me control. I hated my life again. I was alone again. I slid the knife across my wrist once, just gliding it along my veins. I broke down into tears. It was the end of my world. No one understood me. No one understood how it felt to be so confused about life and who I was. I didn't even want to look at myself in the mirror. I was ugly. Everyone else was pretty. Everyone else had it together.

I pressed the blade deeper against my skin, its track indented in my wrist. I shook my head as tears rolled down my cheeks and my breath inched away from me. I couldn't do this anymore. I had to tell him. I had to tell him how unfair this was. I put the knife back into the drawer, making sure it was as neat as my grandmother had left it. I would talk to him first. I would let him know how I felt. I walked up the stairs to the second floor, making sure not to wake up anyone as I tiptoed up the steps, but I heard whispers. My father and stepmother were awake and they were both so excited, but it was so late. Why were they even up?

"We got the house!" My father said. "Khadija is going to be so happy to have her own room. It's so big. This is going to be a big move," my father bragged.

The words punched me in the gut. I held my chest trying to recover. I didn't want to leave. I couldn't leave my uncle. Why were they doing this to me?

I needed to talk to him. He would say the right thing. He would calm me down.

I crawled up the steps to the attic like a cat on the prowl. A cat feeling out its prey, focused, but the darkness caught me off-guard. It was darker than usual. There were sounds. So many sounds, it was as if they were trying to conceal something.

I got to the top of the attic steps and stood there. My legs shook as I heard my uncle sniff so deep it seemed like he'd choke on air. She did the same. They mumbled a bit and then the hard, long sniff happened again.

The bathroom door slammed shut. The shower turned on and I was stuck. I couldn't go back downstairs, but I was afraid my uncle would catch me.

I walked toward the dark figures, taking turns dipping their heads down. I cringed with each step.

My uncle let out a laugh. It was the same laugh he shared with me. I thought I was special. That was *our* laugh, *our* moment. *Why did I have to stay downstairs and be so lonely, while she got to be with him? Why was she even there in the first place?*

"Uncle Trey," I whispered, drawing closer to him.

He still didn't hear me. The fan blew too loud, looped instrumentals creating a symphony of noises on his mastering machine.

The faucet stopped running downstairs, and the screaming water pipes went silent.

I prayed my father wouldn't catch me. I was sure he could hear my every move. I turned back to the two of them and watched as they inhaled white dust.

I looked at her—the crackhead. She had her head dipped down, her body crouched over the table, one finger pressing against her nostril while the other took in the line. There was a bag of powder sitting on my uncle's desk.

He sniffed again, turned toward me, and grabbed his chest, like he'd seen a ghost.

"What the fuck you doing up here?" He said.

His eyes glazed over as he focused on me. I'd never seen him so shook up. I'd never seen him so out of it.

"Sorry," I mumbled.

He wiped his nose, taking in leftover powder residue.

"Cocaine?" I asked. "You do cocaine?"

He cupped my hands in his and looked up at me, leaning into my chest.

"I'm just making sure it's good for a customer. I'll be done in a minute."

I pulled away from him to examine the drug. I reached for it. I wanted to know what the powder felt like between my fingertips. Was it like Pixy Stix?

He slapped my hand down.

I smacked my lips. *How dare he suddenly treat me like a child?* "Let me try it," I asked.

"Hell no!" He said. Look at me!" His face turned to stone as he grabbed my hand. "This shit is nothing to play with. I catch you trying some shit like this and you'll never see tomorrow."

But I felt as if I had nothing to lose. Nothing in my life was going well. Nothing. I wanted to die anyway.

He shook me. "Do you hear me? I'm not playing with you. This shit will kill you. It will kill your dreams and mess up your life. I can't have that happen. I can't. I love you too much. I care about you and I will not be the one responsible for you messing up your life."

He glanced at Marcy. He shook me again. "Do you hear me!"

"Yes."

He grabbed me tighter, desperate for me to snap out of it. He knew I was hurting. He knew when I was being stubborn. "You're fucking with me, Khadija. I know you! Please! I am begging you. Don't get any stupid ideas."

I looked away from him. I was like his daughter and I trusted every word he said. But I also wanted to be like him. I wanted to be smart and charismatic and confident like him and if the powder could do it for him…

"No. No. Don't kill your dreams before you can even get started. You're smarter than that. You're going so far, Khadija. Don't be dumb. There is no coming back from this."

The crackhead looked at me, her sweaty body trembling, her eyes spaced out, unable to focus on the alien standing before her. I shook my head. I would never be like that. I would always have control of my life and she wasn't in control. She was lost, gone. She would do anything for that powder.

I nodded my head, thinking about my future. I turned away from the coke. "I'm moving, Uncle Trey."

He sighed. "I know."

"You knew, and you didn't tell me?"

I was confused. We told each other everything. I knew he didn't want me around because he wanted me to be focused, but suddenly it seemed much deeper.

"You don't love me anymore, do you?"

"Of course, niece. I will always love you. But it's better that you move."

"What? You just don't want me around anymore."

"I do," he said. "You're just growing up."

I eyed him, then looked at her. "No. You're just pushing me away. You don't want me here. You want to be with her."

CHAPTER THIRTEEN

The last trip with my uncle was to Daytona Beach. It was the first time I'd seen a sparkling clear beach, women who wore bikinis as everyday outfits, and heat so fierce, it burned my throat. I held my uncle's hand. I walked the streets with him. He was like a chameleon to me and the coolest uncle I could ever have. He could go from doing coke one night to walking amongst prominent people the next. He could go from speaking as if he were highly educated to making the entire hood laugh. I wanted to be just like him.

"Her name is Dr. Mary Bethune," he said, pointing to her home.

It was a large home, something you wouldn't think a black woman had owned in the early 1900s, but she was special. I could tell by how he spoke of her.

"She wasn't just an activist," he said. "She built Bethune Cookman University, the college I graduated from—a black woman."

I shrugged my shoulders. "Okay. And…?"

He sighed. "Listen. It's one thing to come up with brilliant ideas and theories to change the world, but when you educate people and empower them, and they *actually* change the world, you are a Bad Mamma Jamma."

I wasn't sure if it was the marijuana talking, but I didn't care. His passion for history and determination to make me succeed was inspiring.

I walked inside her home. It was quiet, other than the wood creaking under our feet and the whispers of visitors filling up the cramped rooms. It smelled like old library books. I loved it.

"Hey," my uncle said to a man and his family. "She is going to change the world one day. Yep. My niece. Right here."

My heart dropped as they chuckled. I dipped my head down, covering my face.

I'm not going to be like her, I thought. *Dr. Mary Bethune was bold. She stood up for herself and other people, too. I'm still scared to talk to strangers. Why does he always have to do that?*

But when he said it, he lit up. He spoke with such confidence and certainty, it was as if he had met my future self, sat down with her, and looked up to her.

"I'm telling you," he said. "Lift your head back up, Khadija. Nothing to be shy about."

Something in me wanted to run away and hide, but another part of me started to believe him. I believed and held onto his every word and his belief in me as he strategically built me up.

But it soon became an addiction. When I was around him, I felt as if I could conquer the world and be anyone I wanted—powerful, brilliant, and beautiful—but when he was no longer there, I felt powerless, lost, and unworthy.

We moved one street down from the Heights, a predominantly wealthy Jewish community, but I preferred the hood. I preferred the raggedy streets, loud neighbors, and food from dingy beat-down soul food spots one health code violation away from getting shut down.

We lived in a huge Victorian house on top of a hill. There was so much land around it three other homes could have been built there. I had my own room and could have even had my own little apartment upstairs, but no amount of house could make it feel like a home. I was fifteen, lonely, and everyone around me wondered what had happened to innocent little Khadija.

The next thing I knew, I was sitting in a white room, waiting to be diagnosed.

My father looked at me. His watery eyes begged me to say something. "Khadija. Are you going to answer her question?" He mumbled.

It was too quiet in the room and the stiff leather couch hurt my butt. I felt like I was sitting on a slab of stone; plus, the flowers she had sitting on the end tables made my nose stuffy. I hated flowers. I hated being there, in a room with an old lady, her pen tapping at the clipboard. "Was it the move to your new home?" She said. "What do you feel so depressed about?"

She glanced down at her sheet of paper. "Your father said you don't want to eat. You feel sad most of the time and you find it difficult to control your emotions."

I smacked my lips. *No, old lady,* I thought. *I'm fifteen. Isn't that normal?*

"I am here to help," she assured me.

"Well," I said, slouching deeper into the leather. "I have been feeling a little sick since moving into the house. I have nightmares. Really horrible nightmares of murders - throats getting slashed, shots being fired. It only happens when I'm in the house. And I hear things."

She sat up, clearing her throat. She leaned in closer, her wrinkled face tightening at her lips.

"Really? And this started occurring after the move?"

"Yes," I said with emphasis. "The walls are talking to me. I cover myself with my blanket, but they won't stop."

She leaned in closer, her body stiffening, her eyes growing narrow.

"There was a man there who killed his whole family and—"

"Khadija, stop it," my father said.

"What?"

"You know what I'm talking about."

I shrugged my shoulders. "But it was a good movie. And I think she would really like it. *The Amityville Horror.* We got it for ninety-nine cents at Blockbuster."

The counselor took in a deep breath.

"Do you want to talk to her about the poems I found?" my father said.

My heart beat faster this time. It was no longer a joke. "No."

"About how you wanted to poison certain people and how you wanted to hurt yourself?"

"No."

He pulled my notebook out and immediately, I wanted to snatch it from him. It was a thick, five-subject notebook with torn pieces hanging out. It was as if he was holding my heart in his hands.

"What would make you write things like that?" the woman said.

I grimaced, rolling my eyes, trying to tuck the pain back inside, but the notebook brought back how I felt when I'd written it. I didn't just hate my mother now, I hated my father, my stepmother, and every other adult who tried to get close to me. It was all written in the vilest words I could create. My notebook was my life.

I stared at the wall, studying the paint patterns, and peeled at my nails. I wanted to tell her. I wanted to be set free and regurgitate the turmoil sitting deep in my stomach.

I remember being on the floor. I could see myself in front of a broken mirror. He was behind me. I was naked, and my reflection was split. My face distorted as he moved my body back and forth.

I was seven years old when he told me to come here. I had a towel over me. It was purple. I still had beads of water dripping down my legs when he called me over to him. His hands were big, very big. He told me to open my legs. I did. He smiled. He said my thighs were getting bigger. I eased the towel closer to me, protecting my nakedness. He let me go.

"Nope. Nothing's wrong with me. I just love to write. That's all."

She jotted notes down on her paper and that was it. I never saw her again.

CHAPTER FOURTEEN

I tried my best to be normal and I did a good job for a while, but not being with my uncle kept eating at me. No one could treat me like he did. I went to work with my father, prayed with my grandmother at church, and on the weekends, I bumped my boombox outside with my best friend, dancing to all the worldly music I could consume. Nothing helped, until one day, I found a class I was interested in— Junior R.O.T.C. It was a military class and it pushed me to be the best I could be.

I focused on doing just that. I studied drills in the street, practiced shooting with a BB gun, and led imaginary soldiers back and forth to the corner store. I wanted to move up the ranks and be disciplined like my uncle and stepfather, who were both marines. Each rank I earned made me feel like somebody again, but eventually, it wasn't enough. No one praised me like my uncle. No one seemed to care like my uncle. He was the one who woke me up at the crack of dawn with a gallon of water in his hand. "Khadija! Get up!" He'd yell. "You want to be the best; you gotta run with the best."

He loved me.

My eleventh-grade year, I was ready to move out. I got tired of my father still treating me like a kid.

"Khadija do the dishes, do the laundry, clean your room, and turn down your music."

I turned my Three 6 Mafia up louder.

More and more, I just withdrew myself from everyone, but my father wouldn't leave me alone. He kept trying to find out what was wrong with me.

He started taking me on long rides at night. He'd work a ten-hour shift, pick me up, and try to filter through my silence.

I'd be quiet.

"Come on. You can tell me anything," he said. "I promise."

I looked at him with sadness in my eyes. I could talk to him about almost anything, but not this. I wanted so badly to, but he would say it was my fault. He would just think I was trying to break up the family like before. I wished I was close enough to him to tell him what was really wrong, and why I was so confused about life. I was just too afraid.

"Dad. I want to have sex," I blurted.

I could feel his heart pounding through the seat. He took a deep gulp, as if trying to retrieve his tongue.

"What? Why?"

I'd thrown him off. Now he would leave me alone. I was sure of it.

"Because I do," I replied. "Everyone at school says it hurt, so I want to get it over with."

"What? You're crazy. Why would you do something like that?"

I smiled but was really embarrassed. "For real," I mumbled. "You told me you wanted me to tell you when I was ready." I looked at him, cheesing. "I'm ready."

"You don't want to do this," he said.

"Yes, I do."

"Let me buy you a dildoh. Please," he begged.

"Ew, Dad! No way. That's disgusting!"

He didn't know what else to say. For the first time, I saw him so vulnerable, I thought he would cry. He didn't, but before the week ended, he'd taken as much control back as he could. He took me to the doctor to put me on birth control.

I hadn't lied to him that night. I really *did* want to get it over with. I waited and waited, thinking about it so much it made me even more insane. One day, I finally got up the nerve.

My father was at work the day I wanted it done. It was like surgery to me. I wanted to get it over with; however, I wasn't stupid enough to just get it done by just anybody. They had to have credentials.

All throughout high school, I'd witnessed boys be nice to girls one minute and straight evil the next. The girls would cry in school and get so angry, and for the life of me, I couldn't understand why.

"Girl," her friends would whisper in the locker room. "She had sex with Eric and Ricardo and now they calling her a slut."

And because I had more male friends than girls, I would listen to them talk about how they'd have sex with a girl and then never talk to her again. And if they could get the girl's best friend, they got extra brownie points.

"I bust her cherry and then I said, 'You can go now.'"

And they all would laugh and high five and I would just roll my eyes at their sickness.

I would do much better, I thought. I picked a guy who was a flirt, but he was nice and sweet to me. I was sure he wouldn't tell anyone. I didn't want a relationship; I just wanted it done. I'd protect my heart. When I told him this, he was happier than broke person winning the lottery.

"Brian," I whispered into the phone. "My father is gone. You can come over now."

I shivered that spring day as if I were in the middle of a bitter snowstorm. *What if he's the wrong one? What if he tells his friends and they laugh at me in the hallways like they did Jennifer? She doesn't even talk anymore. Ugh. Boys are so immature.*

"Cool," he said in a caring voice. "I can do that."

He muffled the phone. I laid down on my bed and squeezed my pillow to control my nerves. I wanted to scream. I was scared everything would go wrong. My father would come home early, my neighbor would tell my father, or I'd bleed to death.

"Hello," he said.

"Yeah."

"One second," he said. He muffled the phone again. I couldn't hear what he said, but once he uncovered the phone, I heard his brother yell, "You better tell that hoe come over here!"

"A hoe?" I said. "A hoe?" *Was that what he thought of me? How stupid was I?*

I hung up the phone and never called him again.

After that encounter, my precious goods went up in value. No longer did I feel the need to just give it away. Boys didn't appreciate it and neither did I, until that day. I would wait a little longer and I would make sure it would be with the right person.

This still didn't stop me from wanting a boyfriend. It didn't matter how many As I got, or how well I did in J.R.O.T.C; I still felt a void. I tried getting a boyfriend, thinking it would help, but the conversation always ended up the same. None of them were as focused as me. Their conversations weren't about the laws of attraction or the truths of our heritage; instead, they talked about basketball, Jordan, and Jordans.

I hurt in silence, thinking I should hide forever. I would go to school and be the most focused student, yet I'd come home and sit for hours in the bathroom, contemplating tossing a handful of pills down my throat. I'd lash out at my stepmother and didn't really want to be around my father. I'd lock myself in my room, turn on my Three 6 Mafia, and dream of the day I could escape.

The day would come sooner than I ever imagined—Graduation Day.

PART THREE

My mother cried tears of joy as she watched me walk across the stage. I had made her proud. I graduated at the top of my class, received a scholarship to Ohio State, watched as my entire family welcomed me into the real world, and now I was free. Nothing and no one was going to stop me. I was grown now.

I had so many plans for what I was going to do right after graduation. I was going to get my own place, have an extra room for a library, and turn my car into a tuner, just like they did in *The Fast and the Furious*. I buckled my seatbelt and was ready for this rollercoaster of a life everyone had been warning me about.

"It's not that easy, Khadija. You think you can just do what you want? You're just a kid. Age don't mean nothing. Bills, bills, bills. Just watch. You are going to want to come back home."

Shoot. They must not know me, I thought.

I sat at the dinner table anxiously. I had been waiting for this moment all seventeen years of my life and I couldn't stop smiling because they were going to see. They were going to witness me do big things—without them!

"You're not grown yet," my father said.

I looked at him, puzzled. "What do you mean, I'm not grown? I graduated. You were sitting right there, front and center."

"You're not eighteen yet," he said.

I shrugged my shoulders. "So? I'm still moving."

He laughed. "No. You're. Not. You move out; you're going to jail. Legally, you can't leave until you're eighteen."

I stared back at him. Hurt. What kind of man would do this to his daughter? I'd done everything he asked of me. I took the hardest classes possible, took college classes in the evenings, and held down two jobs. At one job, I was making seven dollars an hour as a tray passer at a hospital. The other, I graded G.E.D. practice tests and assigned their levels in reading and writing. I *was* grown. And people still wanted to control me. It was time for me to do me. That was the number-one thing my uncle had trained me to do. It was my time. I was ready.

"I'm trying to keep you safe," my father said.

"No. You're trying to keep me in your lame-ass house. FOREVER!"

I smacked my lips and sighed.

I'll find a way, I thought, tapping my foot against the couch. *I'll definitely find a way.*

I spent the next couple of days pondering, stressed and ready to just run away. Then it came to me.

"Sign me up!" I said. "I want to join the Army now!"

I had walked a couple of miles to get to the recruiting station. I had come up with a plan—a good one. *So, Daddy,* I thought. *Who's the smart one now?*

It was a brilliant idea and it made the most sense. I had done three years in J.R.O.T.C and I was a great leader. Why not break free from my father's shackles and make money at the same time?

The recruiter looked at me as if he was dreaming. Usually he had to convince people to join, drag them to take the ASVAB, and play the good guy until they shipped off, but with me, I wanted to go, and I wanted to leave on the next train smoking. He signed me up. I took the test and scored so high I could choose any job I wanted. I would leave home—skip college, because that was not what I wanted in the first place—and then I could finally be in control of my own life.

"All right, Khadija. We got you in," the recruiter said.

94

I ran across the office, slapping everyone's hand, as if they were my buddies. "I did it! I am free!"

I was happier than a kid whose parent fell asleep before they could whip them, lifting higher than the clouds.

"But there is bad news," he said.

"What's the bad news?"

"You can't ship out until September."

I stopped, covering my mouth in awe. "Stop playing."

His hardened stare spoke volumes.

"Ah, man," I said, punching the air with my fist. "But that was the whole point of me signing up. I turn eighteen in September."

He shrugged his shoulders. "That's the way it is. It's life."

I walked out, pouting like a two-year old. My plan backfired. I still had to live with my father, but I had signed the contract and the military was about to invade Afghanistan. I was sure to deploy.

I took my broken heart and walked a mile back to my father's house. Nothing ever worked out for me. Life was so hard for a seventeen-year-old. On my way back home, I began thinking of ways to stay away from my father's house. I couldn't stand being at home. By the time I got to my doorstep, I'd come up with another plan. I would work.

I worked double shifts, overtime, and covered as many people as possible. *My father can't control me at work,* I thought. He couldn't complain about anything and I wouldn't have to do any lousy chores. I was gone so much, he barely saw me, but there was one person who did. One person who noticed, the quiet, young girl with cornrows flowing down her back, wearing a mean mug, daring any boy speak to her.

His name was Kimono. Or so I thought.

CHAPTER SIXTEEN

He walked over to me. I rolled my eyes.

"Hey," he said.

His voice was gentle, not hardcore like the sleeve of tattoos inked on his arms. On one arm, it read "PAIN" and on the other, "LOVE." I wondered what it meant. His deep brown skin was smooth, and he carried a glow. His smile was genuine.

"What you listening to?" Kimono said.

Everyone in the cafeteria stood still, observing us, me concealing my smile, Kimono leaning against the counter, totally focusing on me.

I tucked the last spoon inside the napkin. The tray line had just finished and I'd delivered all my trays to the patients. It was almost time to go home.

"Eminem," I mumbled.

I sighed. He was just like Derrick. Just like all the other boys who would do anything and say anything to get a piece of my treasure. I wanted him to go away. He was a bad boy. Bad boys got good girls strung-out on drugs and had them so dumb in love, they'd walk the streets. That wouldn't be me.

"Oh. So, you got the new Eminem?" He said. "How you get it before I did? Let me borrow it."

"No."

"Why you so damn mean?" He said. "All I did was ask you a question."

He unzipped his thick CD case, bursting with all the classics: Nelly, 8Ball & MJG, Tupac, Mos Def, Snowman, and a little bit of R&B, like Alicia Keys.

I reached down under the counter and whipped out my case. It was bursting with Three 6 Mafia, Jodeci, Missy Elliot, Tweet, and Ja Rule. I threw it on the counter.

"Okay. Okay. I see you," he said. "How about we trade then?"

"Cool," I said. "What can I get?"

"AZ."

"Never heard of him."

"Trust me; he's slick."

I smiled, still avoiding the charisma in his eyes. I couldn't let him know that I thought he was cute, but we *did* love the same music. Yeah, he was the bad boy who'd come in late, run his dishwater, and then go shopping down the street as if he weren't on the clock, but he was still cute. He was bold. He didn't care. He wore gold chains and bumped his music so loud in the parking lot, you could feel it vibrating the floors of the waiting room, but he was a gentleman.

Forget about it, I told myself. *You're going into the military. You don't have time for him.*

But as I walked home that day, nodding to the truths of AZ, I felt connected to him. He was different. There was a reason why the girls in the cafeteria flocked to him, laughed with him, and gave up their numbers—or even their panties—to get close to him. He was real, but he still wasn't for me.

I'd watch him from the distance. Kimono. I could stand at my station, folding silverware, and have a straight view of him. The way he vibed to the music, as if it took him to a higher place; the way he gained respect from everyone around him. Yeah. He was a'ight.

Weeks had passed, and I still hadn't given him back his CD. I couldn't. Every time I listened to it, it drew me closer to him. It brought me comfort.

"What's up?" He said, one day.

I pulled the CD player closer to me. I didn't even want Marshall Mathers anymore.

"Hey."

He looked at me and smiled. "I was thinking. I can get your number and we can talk outside of work sometimes."

"No," I said.

He stepped back. "Naw, for real, let me get your number."

"No," I said, sternly.

He glanced at his dude, who was cracking up by the steamer. He looked back at me, as if he couldn't believe I had the audacity to say "no."

"Naw. I'm saying. I want to call you, so let me get your number."

"I said, no."

"A'ight." Then he walked away.

A few minutes later, he came back. He dipped under the table and stood up right beside me.

He gave me chills. I ignored it. He looked me dead in my eyes, gently easing the warm, bulky headphone mitt from my ear. His breath was sweet, his smile wide as the music lifted from my ear. He whispered, "You always got something on your mind?"

"So?"

"What you be thinking about?"

"Nothing," I said, stepping a foot away.

He stepped closer.

"You don't want to talk to me, do you?"

"No."

"Why not?"

I thought about my uncle and how close we had become. I thought about my father, first my hero, then becoming the very one I despised; then my stepfather, who had wooed my mother, then messed up her life.

"You would never understand."

He nodded his head, studying the pain in my voice. I'd never seen such genuine eyes. I stared back, waiting for him to give up, like they all did.

"I tell you what. Write me a letter. I don't want your number and I promise you don't ever have to talk to me again. But I *do* want to know what's making someone so beautiful come in here every day like the world is just a terrible place."

And then he walked away. But I wanted him to stay. I wanted to feel more of his energy. So, I watched him. Just watching him was enough. The big booty girls working in the hospital; they were like the girls in high school, jumping at the chance to get with someone like him. They were more confident, more straightforward, and they loved the fact that I hadn't jumped on his team. *I'm not the kind of girl who would have a boy like that anyway,* I thought. I was quiet. He was outgoing. I was focused. He was fun. *It would never work.*

I couldn't wait to get off work. The fresh air and the lyrics of AZ's *Aziatic*—now my favorite album—allowed me to be at peace. The thought of Kimono lifted my spirits and eased away my worries.

The next day I came in, I held the letter in my hand.

"Where is Kimono?" I asked his friend.

"Kimono?" His laugh echoed off the metal pots and pans and spread throughout the empty cafeteria.

"Yeah. Your friend."

"His name ain't no damn Kimono. It's *Kimani*."

I laughed. "Oh! I been calling him Kimono."

"What's up?" Kimani said, walking right past us.

A wave of anxiety struck me. I was speechless. My heart raced. I handed him the piece of paper and hustled to my station. I didn't want to be around him when he looked at it. I had spilled my guts on that paper—my blood, sweat, and tears.

He took it and for the rest of the day, he didn't even look my way.

I wondered every single hour if he'd read it yet. I watched him vibe out and studied him at his station. Usually, he would turn to look back at me, just so I'd know he could feel me watching him, but this time, he ignored me.

I grew tense. *Maybe it was too heavy. Maybe telling him that I wanted to be free from my father and free to do what I wanted was stupid.* I had all these big goals, but I was truly afraid of the world. How could a girl from the hood make it? And I wanted love, but every man I knew had hurt me. I focused on the tray I was preparing, adding a stale roll here and a salt packet there. *Maybe I need to grow up.* But I was hurting, and I really didn't know why and when someone asked me to write my truths, I gave it my all. I cried through it; I vomited every ounce of being onto that piece of paper. *He probably thinks I'm crazy.*

"Khadija," he said, making his way across the room.

It was the first time he'd called my name. I smiled, feeling that high again. As if nothing else on Earth mattered.

He wasn't smiling, though. He eyed me, then handed me a letter, grabbed his coat, and walked out the cafeteria door.

I tucked the letter in my pocket, trying so hard to focus on not putting sugar on a diabetic plate. I couldn't think about anything but his letter. I came up with all the excuses in the world to leave my tray line to read it—diarrhea, migraine, any debilitating illness. I waited instead.

When tray line was over, I ran to the bathroom. I locked myself in the stall and read it.

Khadija,

I just read your letter and it makes me feel sad. It's crazy to think that all men are the same and that they just want to control you. My mom went through abuse when she was young. I can still remember the stories she would tell me as a little boy. But it made me want to be a good man when I got older. It made me want to show the right woman how she is supposed to be treated. You are beautiful. I watch you sometimes and I hate that you are so withdrawn. You barely smile. I've never seen you laugh. You have to give life a chance. You have to give me a chance. You are going to die one day; why not let go of the past and live? Write me back whenever you need someone to talk to.

When I got back to the cafeteria, I looked up at his empty station. I imagined him there. I wanted to see him and tell him how special he'd made me feel. I barely knew him, but his words had touched my heart. He was a writer. He was deep. I'd never read anything so beautiful. This was impossible. He was supposed to be a gangsta. He looked like one, but his heart...

At the bottom of the paper, he'd scribbled his number. I folded the paper carefully and put it in my pocket.

I ran to the schedule, studying it to see when our days would line up next. I wouldn't see him for another four days. We both had the holiday weekend off for the Fourth of July. I longed to hear his voice. I couldn't wait even one more day.

But if I called him, I would surely be a hoe. I sat home for a day, fiddling with the letter and picking up the phone, just to hang it back up. My whole family was gone on vacation and this was the first time I'd ever been home by myself.

I was seventeen but felt trapped in a thirteen year-old's body. It seemed like everyone I grew up with was out partying at clubs and going to house parties. Me, I just wanted to curl up with a book, listen to music, and study.

I think I should call him.

CHAPTER SEVENTEEN

Everything in me wanted to forget about him, his smile, his laugh, and the special way he looked at me.

Khadija, I told myself. *Don't let it all fool you. Remember what your uncle said about boys; they just want one thing.*

But Kimani's letter just kept running in my mind. *Khadija, just live.*

Those words made me fantasize about him, wondering what it would be like to be with him.

But what if he hurts me? What if he plays me and uses me? I just can't handle it. I just—

I picked up the phone. I called him. I waited.

I should put the phone down. Don't answer. Don't answer.

He answered.

"So, you finally decided to give me your number, huh?"

I chuckled. "Yeah. I guess."

I shook my head. This was it. I was on the phone with the boy everybody wanted. *There go the butterflies again.* But they were wilder than ever, turning my stomach upside-down.

Khadija. Keep it together. You can't let him know. He'll hurt you if he knows that you love him—that you are in love with him. Breathe.

I took in a quiet, shallow breath and exhaled.

"What's your plans now that you graduated?" He asked.

"Well, I was supposed to go to Ohio State."

He paused, as if he were surprised. "Ohio State? You must be smart."

"I am."

"They gon' turn you out," he said.

"What? Never that!"

"Oh," he said, as if regretting his words. "So, you not like that?"

"Nope. I study hard. I'm going to be successful one day and very rich."

"Word?"

"Yep."

I sat down, feeling proud of myself. I was driven and confident in myself and I could tell he liked it.

"What you doing now?"

My heart raced again, and the butterflies would not stop playing "Red Light, Green Light" in my stomach. Each breath I took seemed to lift me farther away into the universe. It was like I was on top of a skyscraper, feeling weightless and free, floating across the sky.

"Nothing."

"How about I come pick you up?"

I thought for a second, looking at my empty house. I'd never had a boy in the house and I really didn't want to get into trouble. But I had graduated. I was grown.

"Okay."

He knocked on the door and I waited a minute before opening. *This is it. He's here.* I paced the floor for a second, trying to tame the anxiety.

I opened the door. He smiled at me.

"Hi," I said, shying away.

"Hey."

His dreamy eyes made me want to just fall into his arms. He looked even sexier in regular clothes. I ushered him in. "This is my home," I said.

He walked in carefully, observing his surroundings. He glanced at my fireplace, adorned with family Polaroids and cinnamon-scented candles.

"Here," I said. "I want you to come upstairs."

I was nervous about it, but I had to do it. I had been dying to share this moment with someone, but I was waiting until it was with someone special.

I was the loner at school, where I was ignored by most boys. No one ever had the chance to see my other side. I couldn't wait to show him.

I grabbed his hand and guided him up the staircase, each step making my heart beat faster.

He stopped in the hallway to admire my prom picture on the wall, then looked at me. "You sure?"

"Yeah. Come on. It's okay."

We made it to my Pepto Bismol-pink room and I pulled him inside.

I was nervous and my voice was shaking as we stepped in. No boy had ever made it past my porch before.

"You see this?" I said proudly. "I'm going to have this one and this one. It comes out in 2004. The new Mustang is going to be raw. I'm getting a red one and maybe even a black one, too!"

I pointed to each car poster and gave him a tour of my toy car collection. I had DuPont car magazines spread out on my bed, peeking out from under my bed and stacked up on my desk. I had circled Lamborghinis, Maseratis, and even some concept cars I vowed I would one day own.

He lit up. "You like cars?"

"Yeah. I LOVE them!"

From that moment on, we were inseparable.

We spent the next couple of days at the lake, chilling on his mother's porch, and we spent our nights in his car, just watching the sunset. We rode around the city like Bonnie and Clyde, seats laid back, banging Big Moe (Chopped and Screwed) down the street. He told jokes; I finally laughed. He introduced me to his family and friends while I shied away. He held my hand. He kissed it. For the first time in my life, I didn't have to wonder what I was feeling; I knew. I had fallen in love.

But I wasn't so sure he was in love with me. He never made it official. He never called me his girlfriend. He never mentioned sex. Most boys would have tried something by now, but he would not go any farther than a kiss.

One day, after work, he took me home. He was dropping me off at the stop sign on my street so that I could walk back up to my house. It was the only way to make sure my father didn't catch me riding with him. Kimani didn't care. He was so ignorant he would have knocked on the door and walked me right inside, but I was still afraid of getting into trouble.

We were almost at the sign when my stomach turned into knots. "Telephone Bill" by Bootsie Collins was playing and a wave of nerves paralyzed me. But I had to ask. It had been bothering me. He couldn't possibly like me like I liked him. I was not like the other girls and he didn't treat me like the other girls. There was surely something wrong with me.

"I don't think you really like me," I blurted.

"Why would you say that?" He turned Bootsie down, slowing at the stop sign.

"I don't know… because you haven't even really kissed me yet."

"That's not true. I do like you."

"Whatever," I said.

I stared out the window, wondering how long this would last. It was just too good to be true. I kept quiet.

He put the car into park, blocking both sides of the street.

"You can't just stop right here," I said with a fiery attitude.

"You think I care?"

I plopped back into the seat, wondering when he would break the news to me. He treated me so well, but he didn't want to have sex with me. That meant he only liked me as a friend. I was one of his boys.

He looked at me and smiled. "You're cute when you're mad."

I smacked my lips and grabbed the door handle.

"Wait," he said.

I let out a deep sigh and turned back toward him. *Just break up with me. I don't want to be—*

I glanced at what he held in his hand and gasped. "What is that?"

He sat the tiny black box in my hand.

"Open it," he said.

I was hesitant. It could be a trick, or a really bad prank, but I lifted the lid anyway. It was a ring. It was a mountain of tiny little diamonds that sparkled underneath the sunlight.

I covered my smile. "For me?"

"Of course."

He slid the ring onto my finger. "This a promise ring. My promise that I will always love you and take care of you - If that's what you want."

I was speechless. I still couldn't believe it. Finally, someone loved me unconditionally. It didn't matter that I still wore ponytails in my hair, almost broke my neck in heels, or that I walked with my head down; he loved every nerdy idea I had, my corny jokes, and the fact that I dressed like I was still a confused thirteen-year-old. He loved me for me.

"Thank you," I said, stepping out of the car. I looked at him. I wanted to stay. I didn't want to go home. I looked into his eyes. He didn't want me to go, either.

"I'll see you tomorrow," he said.

"Okay."

I walked up the hill, smiling so hard, anyone could tell I was in love. I kept staring at my ring, then I looked up at the beautiful blue sky. I couldn't stop smiling. I looked back down at my ring, spinning it so it would sparkle, then I looked up. My father was standing right there. He stood tall, reminding me of Ariel the Little Mermaid's father when she'd got caught with her human.

I put my hand in my pocket.

"Who was that?" He asked.

"What you talking about?" I said.

Kimani's gold chain dangled as I moved closer to my father. I wished I had tucked it inside my shirt, but it was too late. I'd gotten caught. I stared down at the concrete, the little ants running from my feet.

"Give him back that chain and tell him if he's going to drop you off, I need to meet him. No boy should be dropping you off at the end of the street when you have a home."

I looked up at my father with the biggest smile. "Okay," I said.

From then on, all I wanted to do was spend time with him. I switched my days at work to be with him, I walked a mile meeting him at his house at six in the morning just to spend the day with him, and more and more, I didn't care if my dad caught me. I would do anything for him. I would risk it all for his love.

CHAPTER EIGHTEEN

The summer was almost over, and we'd spent almost every day together, but one day, when I walked into his bedroom, I saw a suitcase by the door and clothes spread out all over his bed.

"Where are you going?" I asked.

"Alabama. It's my family reunion."

"For how long?"

"A week."

I frowned, glancing at his clothes and his brand-new Air Force Ones neatly displayed on his bed.

"I want to go!"

I didn't care if he was catching crocodiles in Australia; I didn't want him to leave me, not for one second.

"Let me ask my mother."

He went downstairs on the back patio. "Ma. Can Khadija come?"

"I don't care," she said.

My jaw dropped. I couldn't believe it was that easy.

"Did she ask her father?"

"Shit," I mumbled.

Now *that* would be an impossible feat. My father didn't even know about Kimani. I'd denied I had a boyfriend. Misery came over me as I watched him stuff his book bag with white tees.

I thought about my situation and what my mother used to say to me when I wanted something so bad, but she didn't have it to give. "Where there is a will, there is a way. Khadija, figure it out."

I picked up their house phone. I had an idea.

"Trina!" I whispered desperately.

Trina was my eldest sister from North Carolina, who had also moved to Cleveland. She was a wild and spontaneous spirit.

"Can you tell my dad I'm going to Atlanta with you?"

"Where you going?"

"I'm going to Alabama for a week with my boyfriend."

"Do you trust him?"

"Yeah."

"You sure?"

"Yeah. I promise I will be okay. Please! Please! Please!"

"A'ight. Do you have money just in case you need a ticket back?"

"Yes."

"Cool. Call me when you get to Alabama. And if anything go wrong, you better not let that shit ride. You call me."

"Okay."

For twelve hours, I was on cloud nine, listening to Marvin Gaye, The Temptations, Roger Troutman, and other 70s classics. I sat in the back of the Cadillac with Kimani, while his mother and father sat in the front. We listened to Nelly and Kelly Rowland's "Dilemma", our favorite song, and we held hands, whispering jokes back and forth the entire ride.

But I was the one with the dilemma. I was going to be shipping out soon.

We giggled at each other, giving each other love taps.

We would argue and fight over the simplest things and almost got cussed out by his parents for bringing that riff-raff on their much needed vacation. Nothing could separate us.

The first night of the family reunion, we sat at the table with his parents. They were so cool. We laughed together, ate together, and cracked jokes at his second cousin as he tried to sing Whitney but sounded more like Barry White. We played footsie and couldn't keep our eyes off each other. We ate some of the best fried chicken that night with buttered green beans and indulged in thick cornbread.

"I guess we are about to retire to our room," his stepfather said. I looked at his mother as she grabbed her purse and then his stepfather, pulling out her chair to help her up.

I looked at Kimani.

He looked at me, just as puzzled.

"Where we sleeping?" I whispered.

"We got our own room, I guess."

"What?"

That was unheard of in my world. My father would *neva* let me sleep in a hotel room with a boy. But my father wasn't there.

We slipped out of the banquet and found our room. It had two skinny-looking beds, plump pillows, and a big box TV.

Kimani pounced on the bed like a twelve-year-old boy, while anxiety shot through my body.

This was it.

I couldn't remember the last time I'd felt such freedom from my parents. I snapped my fingers, bringing the memory back. *Daytona Beach with my uncle.*

"Yeah. So, what are we supposed to do now?" I asked.

"Watch TV," he said.

"Yeah, right," I snapped back.

"What do you mean, *yeah, right?*"

I smiled as I began easing my shirt up, showing off my small waist. I was trying to mimic the girls on TV—the strippers—with a seductive dance, but I looked more like an awkward ironing board shuffling back and forth on the floor.

He laughed. "What you doing? Keep your clothes on. Let's just watch a movie."

I just knew he was playing, but then he turned the TV on and for ten minutes, didn't look my way. He waved for me to cuddle under him like we always did, but never did he try to as much as touch me.

I laid down beside him as he flipped through the channels—HBO, BET—and I felt rejected. He didn't want me.

"Can we at least go to the store?"

He glanced out the hotel window. "It's like midnight and ain't no street lights out there. You forget we in the country?"

I batted my eyelashes and poked out my lips. "Please."

"A'ight," he said.

We walked down the street in complete darkness. It was hot and muggy in Alabama, yet I clung to his side. He was my everything and I wanted him to know it. But still, in my mind, there was only one way I could truly show it.

"Get what you want," he said.

I laughed, grabbed a bag of Doritos, then snatched a box of condoms off the shelf. I waved it at him. He frowned.

"Khadija, I don't want to do nothing."

"Why? You have AIDS or something? Got that itchy itch?"

He threw the box back on the shelf, paid for our chips and cookies, and was silent the rest of the walk.

I sighed deeply the entire way back, catching a mean attitude.

Why don't he want me? Boys and men beg for it; they'll do anything for it and here I am, just giving it to him, and he keeps turning me down.

We watched TV all night until finally, he looked at me and said, "Are you gonna pout the whole movie or what?"

I jumped out of bed, pulling my pants down.

"Please," he said. "Put your pants back on."

I could have cried from embarrassment alone. I plopped back down on the bed, threw the covers over my head, and turned the opposite way.

He turned to hold me. "Listen. When I first saw you, all I could think about was how beautiful you were. You were quiet and different than all the other girls. The other girls would jump when I said jump; they would drop their panties when I wanted them to, but you were different. I would show up to their house and they'd answer the door butt-naked, ready for whatever. I could tell them anything and they would let me have sex with them."

I sighed. I didn't understand what he was talking about.

"Every relationship I been in, we had sex and messed it up," he said. "I don't want to do that this time. I want to take my time and get to know you. What's the rush if we gonna be together forever?"

I didn't turn over and smile in his face like the women did in those corny romantic movies. I didn't buy it. I'd never heard of such a thing. He had done so much for me—taking the time to listen to me, taking me places, and being so caring to me, treating me like a Queen—and I couldn't repay him. I couldn't repay him like I'd been conditioned to. Boys wanted sex. That was it. There was no other way to fulfill them.

I got out of his bed and jumped into the other one.

Kimani laughed at me. "You too silly."

He climbed in my bed, pried open my folded arms, and laid down beside me. He held me tight. We stayed in that position the whole night. When I felt his body relax, letting me know he was asleep, I turned around and laid on his chest. Feeling his heartbeat against my face made me feel like an infant on her mother's bosom.

He held me that night and every night of that weekend and that is when I knew he loved me. He was truly different than the other boys. He didn't have to say it; he showed me... but I was leaving.

In three weeks, I would be shipping out. My life was about to change, and I didn't know how to deal with it. I didn't want to feel the hurt. If I stopped loving him, it would be easier to leave. That night was the first time I started pushing him away, picking fights with him, and catching attitudes over the smallest things. I wanted him to leave me, but I longed for him to stay.

Chapter Nineteen

For the first time in my life, money wasn't an issue. I had great credit and money in the bank. We had cars; I had a rusty Cavalier, and Kimani had a candy-blue Bronco with crystals gleaming in the sun. Everything was going so well, almost perfect. *Almost.*

People saw us and wanted to hate.

Our co-worker—a pastor of a church—was in Kimani's ear, telling him that he was too young to settle down and he should leave me, while women in leadership pulled me into their office to warn me to stay focused on my dreams.

I didn't care. Neither did he. We both threw up our middle fingers to the world and on my eighteenth birthday, he parked outside of my house as I lugged my clothes out to the car and we ran away together.

Well, technically, he dropped me off at my sister's house. He was still living with his mother, but it was still we against the world.

Every day, I wished I could run away with him, but every day only drew me closer to boot camp. And that's when it happened.

It was a beautiful summer afternoon. The sun was shining, and the breeze was cool, but I couldn't wait to get to work and make some money. I went in like it was any other day, but I didn't see Kimani. He wasn't in the dish area with his gigantic headphones on, nor was he in the back room stocking food and for some reason, the vibe in the cafeteria was off.

Usually right before tray line, everyone would either be talking while waiting to start or prepping the cafeteria, but instead, people stood around, whispering and shaking their heads. Kimani's name kept coming up. "He got caught," was all they kept saying.

What? I thought.

"They did him dirty. He gone," a woman said.

"What do you mean?" I asked.

But before she could answer, I heard a door slam and a chair crash into the wall.

"Fuck you!" Kimani yelled.

I eased closer to the office and so did everyone else, crowding up the entrance. He walked right by me as if he didn't see me. Then he stopped. He stepped up just an inch from our manager's face and eyed him so hard, we just knew he would punch him. There was silence as their eyes met.

"You a bitch-ass nigga. I should whip your ass," Kimani said.

Security snatched him away, escorting him off the premises. It hurt my heart.

So what if he'd gotten caught driving away with hundreds of dollars' worth of food—ribeye steaks, Boost shakes, and Boston cream pies? So what if he left work when he wanted and spent company hours copping the latest Jordans when he was supposed to be washing dishes? He was a damn good worker. No one ever complained about him when he did his job. Why did they fire my man?

I was pissed. The day dragged without him there. It seemed he took his playful spirit with him. I hated the manager.

"Babe," I said, once I got to his house. "Don't worry about it. I can hold us down until you find another job."

He nodded his head. "Naw. I'm cool."

"No, really. I have money saved up and I can do some more overtime—"

"I already found a job," he said.

He looked at me with sadness in his eyes. He turned away.

"What do you mean?" I said. "Like, why you say it like that?"

"I got a job in West Virginia."

My heart dropped as he shocked me speechless for a second. I couldn't find my words.

"What?" I said. I stood up, barely able to put the pieces together. "What? How?"

"My sister hooked me up with a job out there and I'm leaving next week."

"Next week? When were you going to tell me? You can't just up and leave me like that."

"You about to up and leave *me*. You're going to the military."

"Yeah. But I still wanted to be with you. I still wanted us to be together."

"No, Khadija. You always talk about being free and living your dream. I don't ever want to get in the way of that. I'll just slow you down."

"But you won't," I said.

"It's okay. We can still be friends."

I left his house and went home. I couldn't sleep and no matter how hard I tried to imagine a life without him, I couldn't. He was the one; I was sure of it, but maybe he wasn't. I remembered what my mother had told me when I was a little kid. "If it's meant to be, then it will happen." But then I thought about what my uncle said: "If you don't make it happen, it *won't* happen."

I fell asleep reading Kimani's poems and love letters, feeling his genuine words and how he was everything I'd ever dreamed of. But it was too good to be true. Maybe this was God telling me to go. Maybe he would change after all, like my stepfather did. I fell asleep with his letters surrounding me, but I felt a little bit better.

The next day at work, I wanted to go back home. It wasn't the same. Usually, I would meet him in the cafeteria, lounge around, and we would talk until a manager came to get us. I would pour salt on the table and draw hearts with it. He would beat on the table and rap about whatever I asked.

"You can really make it, Kimani," I'd say.

He'd nod his head and then rap about me inspiring him.

We were best friends.

Every time I looked at his station, I thought about what it would be like to lose him forever. I felt empty without him.

I drove to his house and I rang the doorbell. It was six o'clock in the morning, but I had to get things off my chest. He answered the door. He looked at me, his shoulders slightly slumped. He walked me out to the porch. It was the same two steps we'd sat down on most of the summer, but it would be the last time. I sat on his lap and straddled him. I kissed him behind his ear, holding him tight. He held me tighter.

"What's on your mind?" He said.

I sat quietly, watching a crackhead walk past. It reminded me of Marcy. It seemed the simplest decisions could change the entire course of your life. I took in a deep breath. I had to make the right decision.

"I quit my job. I'm going with you," I whispered.

He pulled away. "No," he said, staring back at me. "I really don't want to be the reason why you don't achieve everything you been talking about."

I smiled, gazing into his eyes. "I am confused about a lot of things," I whispered. "But one thing is for sure; I want to spend the rest of my life with you."

The very next week, I had run away. I was hundreds of miles away and there was nothing anyone could do about it. We lived in our own house in Wheeling, West Virginia and no one knew where I was except my sister and his parents. I was finally free.

"Khadija," my recruiter said, once he tracked me down. "You are not thinking. You are smarter than this. You are just going to let a boy change what you wanted. Your parents think you were kidnapped—"

I smacked my lips. "Well I don't see them trying to find me. And I don't care what you say; I'm not coming back and I'm not going into the military because I was told that as long as you don't get sworn in twice, you don't have to go."

"Who told you that?"

"The boy who kidnapped me."

I laughed.

He hung up.

I felt like a free woman, but once I couldn't find a job, things quickly went bad. We found ourselves sharing a Chinese entree or splitting a foot-long just to make it through the month. There weren't many jobs there and the ones available were too far out and paid minimum wage. It took two months, our car dying on us, and getting pulled over by the police more times than I cared to count for us to realize West Virginia was not for us. We moved back to Cleveland in no time.

Once we touched down, Kimani found a new job working at a factory—Custom Rubbers—while I got my job back at the hospital. It didn't take long for us to live comfortably again.

"We need Direct TV," Kimani said.

He hugged me from behind as we walked through the mall. He kissed my neck and tickled my side.

"No. I don't like contracts," I said.

"We'll pay it," he said. "I promise."

"All right."

"You should get a credit card; then we can buy some new furniture and a TV."

"Okay," I said.

Everywhere we went, I was proud to stand by his side. All I wanted to do was make him happy.

We had everything we could have ever wanted. We both worked during the day, came home, played videos games until nightfall, and then started all over again. We had done what everyone said we couldn't: Survive on our own. We were so proud of ourselves and we were happy.

"Babe," he said to me one night.

We were lying down in bed, talking. We always talked at night. Sometimes with a high, while other times, with a drink.

"I'm getting old," he said.

I laughed. "You're only twenty."

"Yeah. But I don't want to be fifty and too old to play with my kids. I want a kid right now."

I thought about it for a second. He was an amazing uncle. He treated his nieces and nephews like his own. He'd take them to the mall and buy them clothes and shoes and would give them whatever they needed. He made sure that if he had it, they did, too.

Why not? I thought. *Let's have a baby.*

My mother had five kids and it didn't seem that hard. Yeah, she complained about how expensive diapers and daycare was, but she managed. I was only going to have one child.

A month later, I was in the bathroom peeing on a stick, waiting for that second line to appear. And when it did, I saw the most joy I'd ever seen in him. He had fallen in love with it before he even knew what sex it was. I was eighteen; he was twenty. *How could anything go wrong?*

CHAPTER TWENTY

Being pregnant was everything I imagined—except the heartburn, nausea, and the tiny kicks to my ribcage. And Kimani was the best father-to-be I could ask for.

This one time, he would prove it. My stomach was growling and all I wanted in the entire world was some Subway. I wanted double-meat, extra cheese, and have it fully loaded. There was something cool about being able to eat what you wanted when you wanted it just because you held another human in your stomach. I took full advantage.

"Yes, I'm going to eat an entire foot-long," I said.

Kimani laughed at me. He watched as the server piled on the lettuce and tomato, and squirted so much mayo, it turned his stomach. He then sat there as I inhaled the entire thing in minutes.

"Dayum. You sure did just eat it all."

"Yep," I said, proudly.

But by the time we made it to the light down the street, a burning sensation that smelled like onions began rising in my throat.

"I gotta throw up. I gotta throw up!"

We had just got on the highway and the cars speeding past us made me nauseous; the baby was doing flips and I couldn't hold it.

"Pull over. Pull over."

"I can't," he said.

I grabbed the first thing I could find. It was a super-sized Subway cup. I picked up the cup and released all the pickles, onions, and everything else that was mushed in my stomach into the cup. And then it got full. And then it got warm. Just looking at it floating around and the smell coming from the bottom of my gut made me gag even more.

"Here, babe; I can't hold it."

I held the cup away from me and tried giving it to him.

"I don't want that."

"But I can't hold it. It makes me—"

I started gagging again.

The next thing I knew, he'd taken the cup and held it with one hand out the window, while he drove with the other. He held it until we were able to pull off the highway.

"Thank you, baby," I said.

"No problem, baby," he squeezed out, trying to hold his breath.

I was seven months pregnant and happier than ever. I had everything I could have ever wanted and so did my daughter. She was still growing strong in my stomach and had more clothes than I'd ever owned. Kimani had bought her the Jordan 18s, diamond earrings that sat on her princess dresser, and a gold chain to match. Her room was yellow, with Tweety Bird and Bugs Bunny painted on the wall, and between our family, my auntie Berniece, and friends, Melissa and Christine, we had multiple baby showers and everything a princess could ever need.

Yet, all the material things in the world could not fulfill me. I was bothered. There was something missing, something not even my baby or husband could give me. I was having nightmares, back-to-back. They were vivid, horrifying, and many times, I'd wake up paralyzed.

"Babe," I whispered. "Babe."

I was shaking, my clothes damp from sweating all night, and I begged him to just hold me.

He'd wrap his arms around me until I woke up. He would kiss my forehead, his warmth calming me down.

124

"I had a dream," I finally said. "My mother. She was in a casket and she wouldn't get up. She wouldn't answer me. 'Please ma! Get up!' I just kept begging."

Tears rolled down my eyes as I struggled to get the story out.

"And then she jumped up! It scared the shit out of me. Then she chased me.

She chased me around the pews and I think I was the only one who saw her because people wouldn't move out my way. I screamed for her to leave me alone, but she kept trying to hug me. 'Ma, stop!' I yelled.

She stopped. I stared at her. I thought she was going to jump on me or something, but she didn't. She had this look on her face like she was disappointed in me; then she disappeared.

"Babe," I mumbled. "I miss my mother. I really do."

"Why don't we go see her, then?"

"I'm eight months pregnant. It's a twelve-hour drive. I can't—"

"Let's go."

"For real?"

"Yeah. You need to see your mother. The baby will be okay."

I smiled so hard and hugged him so tight. Then I pulled back as a thought hit me.

"But do you think the car is going to make it? It been breaking down a lot."

"Baby. Yes. We'll go next week."

"Awww... I love you."

A week later, he kept his promise.

We jumped into the old rusted Cavalier and prayed every hour. We traveled through the mountains and the snow, and I couldn't wait to jump out of the car to see my mother. Jacksonville had changed so much. There was now a Super Walmart down the street, new schools, new housing, and booming businesses. I grew even more excited when we pulled up into her driveway. I knocked on the door, stepped back, and waited.

No one answered.

I knocked again, listening to the Mississippi Mass Choir sing "Going Up Yonder".

She opened the door.

"Surprise!" I yelled.

She embraced me. She didn't want to let me go. "I can't believe you!" She said.

She looked at my growing belly, rubbed it, and then hugged me again. Her love smothered every bad memory I'd ever had of her.

"You're so beautiful," she said. "I can't wait 'til you come to church so everyone can see how beautiful you have grown."

I laughed, looked at Kimani, and whispered, "Told you so. You're going to church."

She didn't judge me; instead, she pulled me inside, displaying more joy than I'd ever seen.

"Sit down. Sit down," she said.

I sat down on the very couch where we used to watch *The Temptations* and eat shoestring French fries and chewy gizzards, and where I'd dream up the life I would have when I got older. It made me sad. She was living in a double-wide trailer but was still struggling. She didn't tell me, but I could sense it. Through her smile, I could see a whole lot of stress. I looked down at my belly. I'd broken my promise. I was supposed to buy my mother a house. I was supposed to take care of her. I vowed to do it and now I was not able to.

"I'm going back to school," I assured her.

"No, you're not. You need to take care of that baby. No one is going to take care of your child better than you. No one is going to teach her better than you. You stay home."

She looked at Kimani. "Thank you for being good to her. Y'all keep being good to each other. Okay?"

We both nodded our heads.

"I can't believe you are here!" She said.

We spent four days in Jacksonville, went to church, and she showed me off to everyone she knew, from her co-workers to her neighbors. I'd never seen her so proud of me.

I missed my mother.

The next month, I called my mother with baby Armani cuddled in my arms. "Ma. She's here."

I could hear the tears trickling down my mother's throat. "My baby had a baby," she said, before sobbing. "I can't handle it. I gotta go," she said. "I love you so much. Take care of yourself and take care of my grandbaby."

She was so happy and so was my father and stepmother. It seemed everything was going just as we'd planned. We were a family. We were finally complete. Or so I thought.

There was still a broken piece. Me.

CHAPTER TWENTY ONE

It happened overnight. I went to bed one day loving my life and woke up the next day desperate to end it.

I looked at my baby girl, how beautiful and peaceful she was. How she grew into a chunky six-month-old and how every time Kimani opened the front door, she'd jump around, anxious to hear his voice. She was Kimani's everything and he was her world. But I was empty.

My love for them turned into resentment. Every day became a struggle to get out of bed—a struggle to love him, to love her, and even to love myself.

Until one day, I could no longer hide it.

I found myself once again hating everything about my life and once again, I lashed out.

"Just please get out!" I yelled. "Just go! Leave me alone!"

Kimani had just walked through the front door. He wore a smile, held his lunch bag in his hand, his headphones resting around his neck, and he was about to say 'hi.'

There I was, in the living room, once again breaking down, going crazy, and he had no idea why. It was a part of me he had never seen before—the rotting roots of my soul, uprooting itself—and it hurt.

"Who are you?" He asked.

We would have a string of good months, amazing days, but then it would hit me again out of the blue; something would trigger it and punch me in the gut, bringing me down to my knees.

"What is wrong with you, Khadija?"

"YOU!"

I snatched his hand away. I wiped the tears from my eyes, realizing I was crazy, out of my mind, and not even he could help me. I sat on the hardwood floor and cried. My daughter was in her playpen tearing through the mesh, face red, snot bubbling from her nose, and she was crying for me, her arms stretched out, begging me to pick her up. I turned away.

"Just leave!"

"No! Talk to me!" he yelled.

"I'm tired of being broke, Kimani. How do you not get that? I go to work, come home, take care of the baby, cook, clean, go back to work, and then I'm still broke. I'm always taking care of somebody else. I don't have a life. I'm nineteen years old and I can't even go to the club."

"But you don't *like* going to the club."

"So?"

He shook his head as if I were an impossible mission, a monster bursting from its shell. "You're not making any sense. What do you really want?"

"I'm stuck. I'm not who I am supposed to be. I want my life back!"

"And what kind of life was that? A life without me?"

"YES!"

I looked into his eyes and watched his strength being sucked from his soul.

"What do you want from me?" He finally asked.

The look of defeat glared in his eyes as his shoulders fell. "The lights never been turned off. You ain't never went hungry. What more do you want from me?"

"I want my credit back. I want money in the bank. I want you to stop playing video games all day. All you do is come home and play video games. Why don't you go to college and be somebody?"

He stood up just a little bit taller, hurt splintering his voice. "I played video games when you met me. I ain't never tried to change you. I wouldn't ask you to do that. I fucking love you. I love everything about you, but you so stuck on making me somebody else, you don't see it. What happened to you?"

He had this look on his face as if he was tired. I'd seen that look before, from my father. It was one of the worst days of my teen years. I closed my eyes to shut out the pain.

"We used to go to car shows and you used to dream of customizing cars. You loved music back then. You used to smile back then. We were a team. You and me against the world; how could you forget?"

I shrugged my shoulders, as if his words really didn't prick my heart.

"How many rings and chains did I have when you met me?" he asked. "I had amps, a trunk full of sounds, and you thought the shit was cute. Now, every little thing that used to make you smile, you find a way to turn that shit against me. You don't know what you want. It ain't me. It's you!"

I sat there, stuck on his words. I wanted to clap back, but the memories he'd thrown at me wouldn't allow me to deny it. He was right. I'd loved everything about him, from his gentle smile to when he'd turn gangsta on anyone who disrespected him.

I did remember.

Walking through the mall, being proud that he was walking with little ol' me. I didn't care if he blew his paycheck in a day or two, as long as he held me tight at night. As long as he loved me and listened to me and comforted me when I needed comforting, nothing else mattered. It was cool hearing stories of him standing up for people and fighting for his respect; it made me feel like I was with a warrior. He was so confident, and he stood up for himself, something I could not do.

"But things are different now. We got a baby. And I'm pregnant again and you messed up my credit and we living paycheck to paycheck and—"

"I'm going to take care of you. That's what I'm going to do."

"How? You spend up all the money. If it wasn't for you making dumb decisions, we wouldn't be so broke. I spent our very last dollar bailing you out of jail, paying court costs, and getting our car out the impound. I can't win with you!"

He looked at me as if I'd betrayed him. "I missed one payment on the insurance and they locked me up. I can't win, either. I'm trying, Khadija. You know I'm trying."

He walked toward me. "What do you really want?"

"I want more!" Tears streamed down my face and he caught them.

"What's really going on; what happened?" He said.

His voice calmed me. Even when I'd crushed his feelings, he'd try his best to heal mine.

CHAPTER TWENTY TWO

I couldn't tell even him what happened and how it made me feel. I was too ashamed.

Nothing was going right that morning. I couldn't find my keys and my baby wouldn't stop crying. She had never been a baby to cry, but this particular day, she was possessed.

I got in the car and wanted to break down. Yet again, I was on E with only a few coins in my pocket. And I'd robbed Armani's bank just to get that. I was late to my appointment and even more worried I would be stranded on the side of the road. But God kept me. I made it there in one peace.

I pulled the stroller out of the trunk, threw the diaper bag across my back, and rushed into the building. I felt desperate walking to the office. It reminded me of when my mother would walk a mile to the grocery store, her book of food stamps stuffed inside her purse, with groceries shoved in the stroller. Everyone would watch as she walked with all five of her children, some holding her hands, others holding onto the stroller. I hated that I was now walking in her shoes.

I whipped open the door and watched as everyone stared back at me. I must have looked more beat than I thought.

I wore the same wide-leg jeans I had on the other day, Kimani's oversized hoodie, and my hair was jelled back into a ponytail. The office was full of mothers my own age, some pregnant, some with toddlers jumping off their laps.

The pregnant women still had a glow about themselves, fresh manicures, and hairstyles, while the mothers looked worn down from lack of sleep, a bit raggedy from spending every nickel and dime on diapers and daycare, and there I was: nineteen, looking like "Brenda's Got a Baby".

I scribbled my name down on the clipboard and sat next to the other mothers, who looked defeated.

"Khadija," the woman called.

I looked up at her. "Yes."

"Did I say it right?"

"Yes, Ma'am," I said.

I reached down, making sure I'd grabbed everything. *My purse. Bottle. Teething ring. Pacifier.* "I'm ready."

I hadn't eaten all day; I had been in bed, too tired to get up and fix myself a simple sandwich. My stomach growled.

The woman measured my daughter, saying she was longer than most babies. She pricked her finger and left me to soothe her cries and wipe away her tears.

I shushed her the best I could, trying to calm her down, but she was livid, slapping her pacifier to the floor. She stretched her arms out to me. She wanted me. She needed my warmth, my comfort, but my heart had grown cold months ago.

My life was a mess. I was a mess and now I had someone else to take care of. *How did I end up here? How did a girl who was headed to college end up in the W.I.C. office in the middle of East Cleveland?*

Something is wrong with me, I thought as tears welled up in my eyes.

The secretary walked out, and another woman walked in. I looked down at her shadow, trying to hide the tears, trying to keep it together, but it was a battle.

"Khadija," the woman said.

I recognized her voice.

"Khadija, is that you?"

My stomach dropped.

It can't be her. Out of all the people, please, not now.

I eased my head up, smiling as best as I could.

"Hi! Tamika. How are you doing?"

"I'm doing well! How are you? Awww... Your daughter is so beautiful."

I wiped away the last tear rolling down my cheek.

I looked up at her and waited. Tamika was my classmate from high school. We shared notes and worked on projects together in our Honors classes. I couldn't stand to look at her. I turned my attention to my baby.

"Okay," she said. "I have to ask you some questions. Do you have your proof of address?"

"Yes."

"Social. Birth certificate?"

"Yes."

"Are you currently receiving food stamps?"

"Yes," I mumbled.

I glanced up at Tamika, holding my head high, and allowing the tears to fall.

There I was, sitting in front of Tamika, the same girl I bragged to about going to Ohio State, while she was going to Akron U. We'd both graduated at the top of our class, but she went to college and now she was going to determine if I was poor enough to receive Similac for my baby.

135

"One more question," she said, flipping through my most personal information. "This says that you are pregnant with your second child."

"Yes."

I sighed and tortured myself with shame. I had gotten comfortable. Before I walked through those doors, it was okay to be on food stamps. My mother was on food stamps and so was most of my family. Before I saw Sharon's face, it was okay to work the night shift at a factory and come home to barely enough food. It was okay. But as I looked into her eyes, she let me know it wasn't.

I lifted my head up, staring at Kimani. "The way she looked at me," I finally admitted.

"Who?"

"This girl at the W.I.C. office. You should have seen the way she looked down on me."

"You in here crying like you done went crazy because of how some girl looked at you?"

"You don't understand. You don't understand what it's like to get straight-As and make the honor roll every single semester, and then 2 years later to be sitting in the welfare office begging for milk to feed my child."

I pulled away just a little. He pulled me closer. He was much stronger than I. My throat had turned dry and I was becoming a bit self-conscious about the heat in my throat. I turned my head to hide the imaginary scent.

"Come here," he said, reaching for me.

"I think my breath stink," I said.

"I don't give a damn about your breath. Just come here."

He sat down on the edge of the couch. I could smell the rotisserie chicken on his clothes from cutting chicken at his job all day. And his warmth reminded me of who he really was and how much he really loved me. But I knew I was hurting him. It didn't matter how many flowers he brought home or how much he tried to make me laugh or take me out to eat wherever I wanted; something was brewing and every day, it just got a little bit worse.

I walked toward Armani's playpen and pulled her out.

"I just want you to leave," I whispered.

Armani was quiet in my arms. She'd focused in on me, taking in my every word. She reached for her father. I held her back.

"Okay. I'll leave," he said. "I'm going to the mailbox and I'll be right back."

"Whatever."

Armani cried for her father.

He shut the door and I wished he hadn't left. I was scared. *What if he didn't come back?*

I wished I could watch him through my bedroom window to make sure he didn't dip out in the car, but our basement apartment granted no such luxury. I held Armani as thoughts ran rapidly through my mind—my many failures in life.

He was right. It was my fault. I was crazy.

What if he didn't come back?

CHAPTER TWENTY THREE

I rocked my daughter and her warmth comforted me. She was my baby. I was her mother.

"I'm sorry I'm not the mother I should be," I whispered. "I'm sorry for not loving you the way I should—playing games with you and singing you lullabies. I just want to be happy. I don't want to keep struggling and I don't want you to grow up and struggle, too. I will do anything I have to do to make sure you don't end up like me."

She smiled at me. She let me know that it was okay. She let me know that she loved me. She reached out to me and giggled, her big brown eyes sparkling right back at me.

I heard the keys slide into the door and it was a relief. He'd come back. I took in a quick deep breath, wiped the snot from my nose and the tears from my face. I sat up in my chair, trying to frown as best as I could. I turned my attention to my baby, yet I could feel his warmth drawing closer to me.

"Look," he said. "I don't want to fight with you. I don't want to break up, either. I just want my family. I want my daughter to grow up with her mother and father. I didn't have that. And you're right; I make sure she has the best shoes and clothes because when I was younger, I had to fight so people would know that even though I wore Buddies, I was somebody. I don't ever want her to go through that. And I know we don't live in a mansion, but I promise you, I go to work every day thinking about a way to *get* you that mansion. I work overtime because I know that if I can just bring home flowers from time to time, it will put a smile on your face."

I broke down in tears. I remembered those flowers. The flowers he'd bring every week, no matter how much we struggled, until I started neglecting them. I'd let them die in the packaging, right there on the counter, just to remind him of how much money he was wasting.

"I'm sorry," I said. "I'm so sorry. I don't know what's wrong with me. I just feel like killing myself; I feel worthless and I miss my mother. I really miss my mother."

He held me for a second and then pulled away.

"I got something in the mail," he said.

His voice shook as he pulled out a thick white envelope.

"What's that?" I asked.

He let out a deep sigh. "I don't know."

"What does it say?"

He turned the envelope over. It read, "Certified Mail. Open immediately."

I watched anxiously as he tore through the packaging, and as fast as he was birthing the letter from the sealed envelope, it still wasn't fast enough. There was something about it. The seal was like nothing I'd ever seen before.

He yanked it out and immediately, my heart broke. He was going to jail. I knew it. All those years he'd sold drugs when he was younger, the robbery—they were finally catching up with him. They were spying on him. I knew it. My man was going to prison and I was going to be a single mother for the rest of my life. It was happening, just like in the movie *Casino*.

He read it out loud: *"In pursuant of Presidential orders, you are hereby activated for Operation Iraqi Freedom."*

I gasped. "What? Huh? I don't understand. Why would they…?"

My face turned pale and my hands went numb. Dizziness consumed me. I didn't understand. What did they want?

"Kimani Grant, you are hereby ordered to report to Fort Leonard Wood, Missouri on September 11, 2004."

"September? That's just four months from now!"

My heart dropped so deep into my stomach, I had to sit down. I felt nauseous.

"But you can't leave me. You can't go. I can't lose you."

It was just a few months ago I'd cried about my big brother going to Iraq. I had become obsessed with the news. They talked about how the soldiers didn't have the appropriate armor for themselves or the trucks they were driving. They sent them over there unprepared and as a result, hundreds were ambushed and killed. Heads were being cut off with machetes, dead bodies hung from highways, and gunshots rattling in the sandy country could be heard on the five o'clock news.

Almost every day, the American flag came back draped over caskets, thousands being carried by strong soldiers who held a sense of pride for their fallen brother or sister. It made me fear my brother's death.

It was reality. The young child staring at their mother or father's casket, wondering why their heart was in a wooden casket and what happened between the "I'm coming back to you, son," to a silent, lifeless body. And the wife, so weak she had to be carried to the grave alongside the very one she thought she'd spend her life with.

"Nope. You not going," I said. "You staying here."

"I have to go. I'm in the Reserves."

"But you never go to drills and you don't even get paid for it."

"I still have to go."

"But babe," I whined. "I can just shoot you in the leg or something. They won't know I did it on purpose."

A slight chuckle escaped him.

"You can't leave me. You said you would never leave me. We have a family. You see this promise ring you gave me?" I said, stabbing it with my finger. "You made a promise."

"Baby, I gotta go. I signed up to fight for this country. And that's what I'm going to do."

"Why would you do that? Why did you sign up for the military?"

He had this look on his face. Something bothered him, and nothing ever bothered him unless it had something to do with me or his closest family.

"What happened? What's wrong?" I said.

It was rare that he looked defeated, but something had taken him back somewhere.

"Khadija. Shit. It was crazy. I mean, shit blew my mind."

"What?" I said. "What are you talking about?"

He nodded.

I shut up, but it bothered me. Something happened to him. There was a reason why he'd signed up.

Later that night, as we laid down in the bed, he turned toward me, looked into my eyes, and said, "I can't get it off my mind."

"You can tell me," I said. I held his hand. I looked into his eyes.

He swallowed deeply, closed his eyes, and went back to a different time and place. He squeezed my hand and took me with him.

"It was maybe six of us that were back there," he said. "We were on Superior. We had just got off the block and it was a warm summer day.

"Imma call this dude Rich. So, Rich came back there where we were all chilling, looking for James. James was just a dude who hustled with us on the block.

"So, Rich was like, 'I ain't got no problems with none of y'all, but with this nigga right here. All I want is a fair fight.'

"It was the beginning of the school year because the bell had just rung, and we were right across the street from the school, but in the back.

"We was cool with them fighting. It was their beef, so whatever.

"Rich squared up with James, they swung a couple of times, then Rich caught James in the chin. His knees buckled. *Boom.* He hit the ground. That was the end of the fight. He lost that one. We helped James up and he got his self together. He was like, 'Naw, fuck that nigga,' and so he went and charged back at the dude.

"They squared up again. Then Rich caught him again and laid him down. *Boom.* So, after that, we were like, 'He done had enough, just go 'head on.' So, by this time, the fight done made its way from the back of the apartment to the side, so now we in the driveway, directly across the street from the school.

"James' car was parked in the back. James got up and was like, 'Fuck that nigga. Fuck that nigga.' And he ran to his car. At that time, we really didn't know exactly what was up.

"Rich was walking off and we thought it was over. James came back with a thirty-eight in his hand, a little revolver. He grabbed the gun and my other dude was telling him to put the gun down. At that point, you knew something bad was going to happen. You could look at his eyes and tell. And old buddy seen it, too. It was like he *knew*. When he seen it, he started running. He made it to the middle of the street, but James was chasing him down. He let out one.

"He missed.

"He let off the next one and by the time he shot off the third one, you knew he had hit him. Dude had just crossed the street, right there on the median. Little kids were walking down the sidewalk because school had just let out.

"He let out the fourth one and the dude dropped dead right there in the middle of the street. He didn't move. Like, it wasn't no nothing after that. He didn't move. Everybody kind of stopped, like, 'Oh shit,' like, 'He really just killed him.'

"It was like, a moment of silence, then after that, everybody dipped out. I went straight to the house. I got to the house and I was like, 'This shit ain't for me.' The next day, it was cloudy outside; it was gray as fuck and I'm like, I need to do something. The police was throwing everybody on the block in jail to figure out what happened. I wasn't saying shit. The only thing I could think of was a marine recruiter who walked around the high school. I walked up to the recruiting center and I walked right into the office, saw the dude, and was like, 'Yo, I wanna sign up.'

"I still had twelve-hundred dollars in the streets. I had four in dope, another five that my dude owed me—that I had to pay back to the dude who *gave* us the dope—and some fiends who owed me. I ain't care about none of that shit. I got my money back from my dude, I paid the dude we owed, and I washed my hands. Six weeks later, I went to boot camp."

I couldn't believe it. He'd been through a lot, but kept it all to himself.

"I'm so sorry, babe. Why didn't you ever tell me that?"

"There is a lot of things I don't tell you. I can't have you out here worrying about me."

"I just feel like I'm always stressed, but you hold it all in. I wish I knew, so I could help."

"You're good," he said. "Just take care of yourself and my babies. I need to concentrate on getting back to y'all."

Three months later, we kissed at the altar. The whole family was there—rather, *his* whole family was there. I didn't invite my mother and I didn't even want my father to walk me down the aisle.

I had on my prom dress, Kimani wore his father's oversized blue Easter suit, and we exchanged our thirty-five-dollar wedding rings.

Our honeymoon was at Dave & Buster's—an arcade—and then we spent the last week preparing for our final day together. It came fast.

Eleven days later, I sat at the gate with him, waiting on his flight. Every minute brought me closer to breaking down. I prayed for a delay; I prayed for a pardon, but the plane ran on time and no one made that one very important phone call that would have let him stay home.

"Dada! Dada!" Armani shouted, reaching out to him.

But he had to keep walking. He had to turn away and ignore it.

"You be strong!" He shouted, right before disappearing onto the ramp.

"Okay!" I yelled back.

For the next two weeks, I stayed in bed while my daughter cried. I couldn't get up, I didn't want to eat, and I didn't have the energy to feed my own child. I moved back in with my father, then spent a month with my mother, but knowing I might never see Kimani again tore me apart.

What am I going to do now?

CHAPTER TWENTY FOUR

I did what Kimani told me *not* to do. Soon, I couldn't take it anymore. I became desperate. I needed to feel close to him.

I searched for the two envelopes, the ones he had tucked away just in case of an emergency. It had been a week since he'd boarded the plane and I had still not received one phone call from him. It was definitely an emergency.

I jumped out of bed and ran to the dresser. I yanked the drawer open and searched for the letters. They were letters I was only supposed to read if he didn't return. One was for me, and one was for Armani and my unborn child. But I couldn't wait. I tore through the envelope, pulled out the letter, and slowly took in every word.

If you are reading this, I am probably no longer physically with you. But I will always be with you. From the first time I met you, with your headphones on, listening to Eminem, I knew you were different. You turned down every dude who tried to holla at you. You were focused. I know you probably think you can't handle it, but baby, you are one of the strongest women I know. You are an amazing mother. You don't think so, but I know you are. So be that amazing mother. Be that strong woman with big dreams and that 'I'm going to go get it and no one is ever going to stop me' mentality. You are everything a man would ever want. So, just because I'm gone, don't lose that fire. You were whole when I met you; you just needed me there to remind you.

"I'm sorry!" I screamed.

My legs weakened, my head spun, and nausea rose to my throat. I climbed back into bed and curled up in the fetal position.

"I miss you!" I whispered, as if he were there. "You were the one that saved me from myself and I pushed you away. I cry every day for you, baby. I cry every night. Armani is crying for you, too. You have to find a way back to us. You always find a way. Please don't die. Please come back to me!"

I then launched into a desperate prayer. "God, I don't know what I would do if I never saw him again. Please protect him. Please bring him home."

Then it hit me, like a lightbulb had been turned on. *Ding*!

I jumped out of bed like a madwoman. *He was right!*

Anything I had ever put my mind to somehow always came true. I didn't know if it was because of my mother praying for me or all those years I went to church, but I had something my church family would have called, "favor."

A burst of energy shot through my body and suddenly, I had all the clarity in the world. "I can't give up! I *never* give up!"

I grabbed my baby, bundled her up in the blanket he'd left for her, jumped in my car, and threw it in reverse.

31, 24, 49, 35, 6, 5, I kept chanting. I held onto those numbers as if they were my life.

She's crying again. My nerves were shot, and I needed Armani to be quiet.

"Shhh," I said. "Mommy needs to remember these numbers. Be quiet! Please! This is our only chance."

31, 24, 25, 34, no, 32.

Why didn't I just write them down?

I glanced at the clock as I swerved into the parking lot. It was 6:57. I pulled Armani out of the car seat and sped ahead of the line.

"I only have one minute left," I begged the cashier. "Please hurry. My husband is in Iraq and if I can just win this ticket, they'll let him come home."

The Indian man stood there for a second. "What?" He chuckled, his thick accent confusing me.

"Just play the numbers, please!"

I snatched the printed ticket and rushed home. I threw a bottle in my daughter's mouth and rocked her. I focused hard on those numbers as they flipped inside the bowl. I believed with all my heart I would win. I just had to. I prayed the numbers would come through. I talked to them, thinking that if I just focused hard enough, I'd win.

"25," the woman called out.

I looked down at the ticket. Even though I knew the numbers, I wanted to triple-check.

"Yes! The Lord hears me."

"46, 5, 6."

My heart dropped, and the tears fell. Just like that, I had failed him. I couldn't come up with the numbers that would bring my husband home.

For the next month, I studied every Mega Millions winning number for the past year. I needed to play strategically. My husband's life depended on it. I spent more time researching past lottery winners, their rituals, and their lucky numbers than I did holding my child. I loved her to death, but I was trying not to go crazy. We played games, and I read her books, but I was too busy holding onto the next day I had a chance to win and see my husband return home.

My madness came from an article I'd read. It said that rich people were getting their daughters and sons out of going to war. I wasn't rich, but if I won the lottery, I had a chance.

I spent three-hundred-and-fifty dollars before I realized I had failed. I had even written Oprah and sent her a picture book of Kimani and Armani, asking if she could do something. It was impossible. There was no way I could get my husband home.

I cried until I was so dehydrated I didn't have the strength to pull myself up out of bed. My daughter had been crying for hours. She was hungry. She was missing her father, his touch, his smile, and I couldn't handle seeing the hurt in her eyes.

"Khadija," I heard my father say.

I pulled the covers over my head. I didn't want him to see me so debilitated. My eyes were so swollen and dry from crying, I could barely open them. I hadn't taken a bath or brushed my teeth in days, and dirty clothes and diapers were scattered all over the floor.

"I'm okay," I said.

He walked in and sat on the edge of the bed. He pulled the covers back. "Get up," he said.

"I don't feel like it."

"So what? Get up."

I snatched the pillow from under my head and covered my face. I cried.

"Khadija. Look at your daughter. Look at her."

I looked at her as she sat in her crib, her hands gripping the wooden bars. She had stopped crying, but her face was red, and snot had crusted under her nose.

I covered my face.

"No," he said, snatching the pillow from me and throwing it on the floor.

"You look at your daughter. She is only going to be as strong as you are."

150

I pulled myself up and looked at her. She was a mirror image of me. Her tears came from me, her fear came from me, and as she sat down behind those wooden bars, I realized she was in prison, just like me. But she could get out and so could I. She'd done it before. She'd used a pillow and stuffed animals, stood on them, and pulled herself out. She was too busy watching me wallow in pain to think about how close she really was to her freedom.

I took a deep breath.

"Can you just take her and feed her, and I'll get her in a couple of hours? Please."

My father smiled. It was the same smile he'd given me when I was determined to be Sanaa Lathan in *Love and Basketball*, dribbling the ball up and down the driveway for hours on end. It was a beautiful smile, with a deep dimple on each side.

He reached in and grabbed Armani. She threw her arms around his neck and held him tight. I blew her a kiss.

I was by myself. For the first time in my life, I was by myself. Kimani wasn't coming home before his date. I could no longer deny it.

I glanced at his picture, thinking about the good times we had driving up and down the streets of East Cleveland dodging potholes, the long nights eating ice cream and playing videos games, and even the night neither one of us could ever forget.

CHAPTER TWENTY FIVE

I grabbed a pen, then found a notebook. I didn't even think about it. The images were so vivid to me; the memories kept coming, flashing like I was watching a movie screen, and then I could feel him. I could hear him there with me; I could hear his voice. I wanted to write.

I remembered that energy—that need to write, to get my thoughts down—but I had lost it a long time ago. I had no idea where it came from, but it began to fill the emptiness.

The words purged out onto the paper and I didn't care how it looked or even if I could read it. It felt good to be free.

Kimani. Baby. I miss you, so I decided to write you a story. Hope it takes you back :) I hope you like it!

It was a late night. No, it was about two o'clock in the morning. I was lying down naked, my small baby bump nice and warm. You had gotten out of the bed. I could feel when you left me, but I was still asleep, tucked under the covers.

"Khadija!" You yelled.

I grabbed my chest. My heart hurt. It was beating too fast and I could barely catch my breath. I was confused. I'd forgotten where I was.

"Khadija, get up right now!"

I looked at you. I'd never seen such fear riddling through you. It was pure fear, danger.

Someone must have been there. You had just re-upped your weed stash and maybe someone was there to rob us.

I snatched up a t-shirt and threw on some shorts. It was the first thing I saw. Our pit, Monte, wouldn't stop barking. His bark was loud, aggressive, a warning. That's when I heard someone screaming—a man outside screaming and yelling for his life. My stomach dropped. What in the world was going on?

I kept trying to ask you, but you kept telling me in a rushed, nervous voice, "Come on! We gotta get out of here!"

I wobbled into my shorts and ran out of the bedroom door into the living room. And that's when I saw it. A fire, flames consuming the porch, blazing so hot, the glass door shattered to the floor.

I wanted to scream. I wanted to run. I couldn't believe it. It was happening to me. I'd seen people lose everything, but never did I think it would happen to me. Everything I'd owned was about to be gone. I couldn't think about grabbing anything, though. I held my baby bump, running down the long hallway to get to the exit, praying to God that running so hard and so fast wouldn't harm it. It was a long hallway, forty apartments long. But we didn't even know which way was the right way. Where was the fire coming from? What if the floor caved in as we were running out? Lord, please. We followed God. He led us out the right way.

"Fire!" We screamed, trying to warn the other neighbors, banging on doors and kicking the walls of the hallway. The fire alarms didn't go off. They weren't working. The building was four stories high. There were children in that building, grandparents, and babies, and we were scared for their lives.

"Get out the building!" We yelled.

We made it outside. We watched others peel from their apartments and we stood there. We held each other, and we stood there and watched as the wood and everything in the apartment caved under pressure, heard the cracking and the cries and the screams, smelled everything burning, saw the ashes floating through the air.

We then saw the man who we first heard screaming. His entire arm was bleeding, flesh raw to the bone, and he kept saying, "I'm sorry. I was frying some chicken and fell asleep."

"You was high, mothafucka!" You said.

The man turned away in shame. The ambulance came, the Red Cross came, and suddenly, life was more precious than anything money could buy.

We stayed in a hotel that night and all I could think about was how crazy our luck was. We were too young to lose everything we'd worked for, even Armani's brand-new stroller.

Remember that stroller? How that crackhead broke into my trunk and stole it and I had to buy another one?

I remember walking back into the house a week later. There were holes in the walls from the firemen searching for flames, our furniture was turned over, and our clothes were everywhere, but nothing was burned. Soot covered almost everything there, but at least we could clean it. I remember flipping through my prom pictures and family Polaroids and thinking, 'Thank God.'

There was nothing except the beams and metal framing left in the apartment downstairs from us, yet we didn't lose a thing.

I exhaled as I wrote down my last word. It was a familiar place. I'd remembered that exact feeling, that feeling of losing myself so deeply in something, I had forgotten where I was. Nothing or no one else mattered and I missed that. Something inside of me needed that.

I saved the document under Memories of Us and emailed it to him.

I couldn't wait until he could read it. *But what if he didn't like it?*

He read it, and replied:

You are a damn good writer. When I read your story, I forgot about this sandy, hot ass place. I forgot the uniform I wear, and I felt like a father again, a husband. I let my dude read it, too. He said it was cool as shit. Can you keep sending them to me?

It didn't take long before I had turned the news completely off and focused on what I *could* control. I was thousands of miles away, but I could write stories that could take his mind off mortars and IEDs, even if it was just for twenty minutes. It empowered me, knowing I could do something.

I began taking Armani to the park, helping her learn her numbers, and introduced her to the library. It was my mission for her to see herself in me -Strength.

Imani, our second baby, came a couple of months later. She was just a week old when Kimani came to hold her and love on her before having to go right back to war.

"She's so beautiful," he said. "I swear, I am so blessed."

He moved me out of my father's house and I was able to get my own place. And when he left, my heart broke again.

"You seem like you are doing much better," my father said.

"I am," I said, smiling.

"What happened?"

"I don't know. I guess being by myself; I'm starting to learn more about who I am."

"Oh, really? So, now you see why I didn't want you having a boyfriend too early."

I laughed. "Yeah. I get it. I understand. You don't have to say, 'I told you so.'"

"I won't," he said. "But I did."

We both laughed.

Eighteen months later, my husband walked off the plane. It was the most nervous I'd been in over a year. So much had changed, but I had been waiting on that moment. I waited and waited, hoping he would still think I was cute. I'd had a baby and looked a little different.

I finally saw his plane land. My heart sped up as I heard people clapping and cheering. And when he stepped off the ramp, I fell in love again.

CHAPTER TWENTY SIX

"I missed you, baby!" I yelled, throwing myself into his arms. "You can't leave me again. Promise me, you won't leave me again."

Tears rolled down my face as I looked into his eyes. He lifted me up, his arms stronger than I'd remembered, and he kissed me.

His lips were foreign to me. It felt like the first time we met. Our first date. Our first kiss. The butterflies went wild deep in my stomach and his heart beat so fast, I could feel it through his chest.

"I promise," he said. "I ain't going nowhere."

He smelled like a military man, like he'd been working on planes or been outside, building something. He walked like a military man, too. I loved it.

"I missed you so much!" I whispered, holding him tight throughout the airport.

People stopped and stared. They gathered around him, bought him drinks, and every turn we made, they thanked him for his service. The news was there to headline the next featured article, *"Hometown Hero, Specialist Kimani Grant."*

"I can't wait until you see the girls," I said. "Armani is big now and Imani, she is so beautiful."

I couldn't tame my smile. I walked proudly with my King.

Once we left the airport, the entire ride home, we sat in the backseat and listened to the songs we could only talk about over the phone.

"Babe, you have to hear this new song by Jennifer Hudson. Every time I listen to it, I think of you," I said.

"Naw, man. You have to listen to John Legend, 'Get Lifted.'"

We listened to John Legend's 'So High', held hands, and whispered in each other's ears as his father drove us home.

He was so excited to get home. He stared at Browns' Stadium as we crossed the Cleveland Bridge, smiling at the flashing lights of the skyscraper, Tower City. His hands shivered.

"I'm scared," he said.

"Why?" I rubbed his hand, brought it to my lips, and kissed it.

"What if they cry when they see me? I mean… do you think they even know I'm their father?"

"Of course," I said. "They know."

His hands shivered more the closer we got to the house. I gripped his hand tighter.

"It's okay. I promise."

He walked through the door like a stranger in the house. It seemed like everything was new to him again.

"Daddy!" Armani yelled. Her eyes grew big and bright and her smile warmed everyone's heart. She was a Daddy's girl before she left, and his presence had never left her.

He knelt down on one knee and wrapped his arms around her. "You called me 'Daddy,'" he said. "Yes, baby girl. I am your daddy." His head dipped down before her as tears eased from his eyes.

He held Imani, who he hadn't held since she was a week old. "I'm here now," he kept saying. He rocked her, staring at her, cherishing every second he had her in his arms. "She's so big now - Nine months. I missed nine months of her life," he said. "Daddy won't miss anymore. I promise."

He'd missed Imani's birth, he'd missed Armani's first steps, but the way he held them, I knew he would never leave them again.

"I feel like a celebrity," he said.

"You are. You are a hero; a warrior, and I am so proud of you. I can't believe you are back. It's unreal."

For the next couple of weeks, we were inseparable. I woke up with him, cooked him breakfast, and catered to my King's every desire.

We reminisced by visiting the hospital where we'd first met, driving to our old neighborhoods, listening to Ludacris and Usher's *Confessions* like the old days, but I could tell something was wrong. I could tell at the airport, the very first time I looked into his eyes, that a part of him was missing.

"You all right, baby?" I asked.

We had spent an hour in the car, just listening to music and riding around and suddenly, he went quiet. He stared into space while driving, completely zoned out, and then looked around, as if watching his back.

"Babe. Are you okay?"

"Yeah," he said, with a forced smile.

A month passed and as he retired his uniform, he became less and less excited about life. He talked more about his battle buddies and how he had grown close to a soldier and then lost him. How he'd almost lost his own life to a mortar and when he'd gotten lost between Bagdad and his military base.

"What would you say if I went back?" He said.

"What? Why would you do that?" It hurt that he would even utter those words. "Why would you want to leave?"

"They got contractor jobs over there. I can make a hundred grand a year. I can come back, buy us a house, and then you wouldn't have to work."

I glanced at the man who was once vibrant and ready to get out and go and who'd laugh and had fun. I held his hand.

"Are you okay?"

"I was a hero in Iraq," he said. "It was me and one other person on a mission for months at a time. I was responsible for somebody else's life; I was a leader, but here, I'm just another black man getting harassed by the police. Without that uniform on, don't nobody give a shit about me. I don't belong here. I had purpose over there; nobody cares what you did or what you been through."

"You *are* somebody. You are everything to me."

"Of course, to you. But over there, I was somebody who had a purpose."

The sadness he'd shown, I'd never seen before. He was so disconnected, playing video games more and sleeping to pass the time. I wondered what had happened over there, but he would never tell me. He'd just hint at things, keeping them a secret, but as his dreams of Iraq interrupted our nights, his body trembling, me climbing on top of him to calm him, I knew something was wrong, but I also knew that just like he was always there for me, I would now be there for him. We against the world.

CHAPTER TWENTY SEVEN

Six months later, we were back on food stamps, jobless, with no medical insurance. They cut everything off with not so much as a warning.

With a growing family, the pressure was on to find a bigger place and get back on our feet.

We started making moves. Kimani started working at a factory; I started going to job fairs and putting in applications and then we decided to rent my father's house. We were determined to create a good life for our children and this was a great start.

I was proud of that two-story home. I dipped my head in and out of the rooms and planned how each room would be used. My daughters would have the second dining room filled with more toys than any two-year-old should ever have and the attic would be turned into a studio. The kitchen had brand-new granite counters, flooring, and cabinets, and everything smelled like fresh drywall. There were enough bedrooms for each of our children to have their own space and we had a gigantic room where I could watch my "MTV Cribs," "Fabulous Life of Kimora," and "True Life". In the living room was a fireplace. It was our first house, our first big step in life.

Once we moved in, everything went according to plan. We watched movies on a big sixty-inch flat screen TV, with surround-sound that kept the neighbors up all night. Family would come over, have drinks, and my husband and I would dance in the living room to T-Pain's "Studio Luv" and R. Kelly's *TP-2.com*.

It was a house in the hood, on 134th street off Hayden, just a street down from where Bone Thugs grew up, but it was ours.

I found myself standing in line at the welfare office once again to get back on W.I.C. and get my babies back on Medicaid. But this time, my pride went out the door. I didn't care what line I had to stand in to ask for help, as long as my husband was standing beside me. He, on the other hand, hated it. Every time we'd swipe the card for free food—no matter if it was steaks or peanut butter and jelly—it hurt his heart.

"I want to be able to take care of my family," he said. "I don't want you to work. I don't want my kids in daycare. I'm a man, and men should take care of their own."

But I wanted to work and couldn't wait to find a job. Plus, the girls were going to spend a couple of weeks with my mother, so that meant I could work all the overtime I wanted. And that's when I met Mrs. Randle.

The woman was a petite, stunning grandmother. She had long, silver hair and a beautiful smile. "Do you know how to weld?" She asked.

"Yeah. I did a little welding at this temp agency."

"Sounds good," she said.

I ran through my laundry list of temp jobs and how I'd worked at different factories and was proud to have almost gotten hired at one. I loved factory work. I was good at it. While most people hated repetitive work, I thrived off it. I made anything from plastic to metal car parts, photo albums, and even book covers. Anything that would allow me the opportunity to be by myself, zone out, and do me, I was down for it. I could out-produce any man in the building and even thought about making a career out of it.

"I'll refer you to our HR department. Come in tomorrow at noon."

At the interview, I practically begged for the job. "Please," I said. "I will be the best worker you've ever seen. I'll always work overtime, anytime you need me to. I come on time every day, and I will even peel the old tape off the floors on my downtime."

"Can you carry forty pounds of metal hoses from one section of the factory to the other?"

I stood up straight as if I were a private in the Army. "Yes, Sir."

"Can you work from seven in the evening to seven at night?"

I thought about it for a second. Imani was only a year old. I didn't have daycare, so that would mean I would have to get off work in the morning and still tend to her.

"Can you work those hours?"

"Yes, Sir."

"Then you have the job." He shook my hand and pointed me to my workstation.

"Be here at 6:30 PM and Reggie will teach you what you need to know."

I was excited about my first welding job and proud. I was making eleven dollars an hour. That was more than I'd ever made before.

I came in from the dock area and was welcomed by the woman who'd referred me. She gave me a tour.

"You *do* know that you are the only female working at night. Are you okay with that?"

"Yes," I assured her.

"Is your husband aware of it?"

"Yes," I lied.

"I didn't know you were working the night shift. Please let me know if you have any issues or concerns."

A man walked up to us.

"Let me introduce you to Reggie," she said.

"Hello, Reggie." I shook his hand.

He was a tall, muscular man with gray stubble growing roughly around his chin.

"Reggie is going to take it from here. Reggie, this is Khadija. She has some experience with welding, but she is not familiar with orbital welding."

"No problem," he said.

He smiled, happily, until the woman turned her back. He then morphed into the Grinch.

"What made you want to work here?" He said.

"I like factory work."

"Why you working here in the middle of the night though? That's not smart. Don't you think that's dangerous, working with all these men? Most of them are felons, can't get hired anywhere else, and here you are, a beautiful Queen working with the toughest men on the block."

"Queen?" I said. "I'm not a Queen and I'm not scared of them."

"Disregard," he said. "So, why you want to weld? … Oh," he said, slapping his hand onto his head. "Massa offered you a deal you couldn't refuse."

I frowned. I put my hand on my hip. "What are you trying to say?"

I rolled my eyes and sighed. If he was going to be my trainer, I was going to be in big trouble.

"I'm not trying to say nothing. I'm telling you to get those hoses over there, drag them all the way over here, and I'm going to teach you how a real good slave do it."

Every time I saw Reggie or even heard his voice, I cringed. He was the worst trainer in the world. I couldn't do my job without having to listen to him all night long, "Go 'head, girl. You gon' be nice and strong for Massa when you get done. Your back ain't gon' be no good, but you sure gon' make Massa some money. He gon' be proud."

He'd almost bring tears to my eyes as sweat gathered on my forehead. It was like carrying forty-pound snakes and dragging them from one part of the village to the other. The only difference was, metal pieces would catch in my clothes and cut me up all night. I still didn't mind my job.

RING. RING. The bell rang.

"There you go. Lunchtime. Fifteen minutes," he said. "Go fetch your scraps and be back in time to make Massa some mo' money. What time is it? It's midnight. Massa in his mansion sleeping good with his beautiful wife. You? You can't even spend time with your family because you too tired busting your ass in here with me every day."

"Shut up!" I said, finally yelling back at him. "You sound so damn bitter. At least you got a job."

He'd ignore me every time. "When you going to go back to school? When you going to work for yourself? Tired yet?"

I thought about what he said. It did seem easier to just go to school and become a nurse. At least the pay was better, and I could see my family. I shrugged the idea off. *When would I have time for that?*

"Nope," I said. "I ain't tired."

A few months after working there, I went in tired and exhausted and the last person I wanted to see was Reggie. I threw on my apron, punched my time card, and was met by my supervisor.

"Eh," he said. "You have a new trainer: Brian."

I looked at the old man and then back at my supervisor.

"Where is Reggie?" I asked.

"He passed away last night."

RING. RING. The bell went off again.

The workers rushed to their stations as I stood there paralyzed. They hadn't even noticed Reggie's absence, nor did they stop to care.

"I know it may be hard for you," my trainer said. Every day, it seemed y'all were talking about something. Sorry about the news," he said. "Tell me. How much have you learned on the welder? Show me what you know."

With tears welling in my eyes, I grabbed an armful of hoses. I strung the heavy metal against my back and I pulled them along the concrete floor. I could hear Reggie. He was in my ear. *When you gonna drop them hoses and pick up a book? Any book that will tell you how to get the hell out of here?*

"I can't," I whispered back.

Yes, you can. You told me about your dreams. You're young. You're smart. Ain't nothing wrong with you but that fear in your heart. Get up off your ass and build. Build for your mother. You talk about helping her every night. Build for your daughters, so they will never have to work their fingers to the bones for ten dollars and fifty cent an hour.

From that day on, I wanted more. I could no longer settle. I had a dream to become a big time CEO or run my very own business and be able to see my kids whenever I wanted, but I didn't know what I wanted in life. I did know that every day I walked into that place, I should have expected more from myself. Reggie was right. He had made me mad many nights and caused the hours to drag slower, but he had been trying to get me to see something.

After he died, I finally woke up.

I used every break I had to jot down ideas. *A web designer. A nanny. A psychologist, a teacher. Anything but this,* I'd write.

And then, between the welds, I'd jot down short plots for stories. I was determined to break free. Everyone looked at me as if I were insane, jumping from the machine to my notepad, writing furiously. But, I was the only one smiling. I had big dreams and I was going to do something about them. The only problem was, I didn't know where to start.

But I did have this one idea. I went home and couldn't wait to tell my husband.

"Babe," I said. "I got an idea."

"What's that?"

"You love motorcycles, right?"

"Yeah."

"I mean, you *love, love, love* motorcycles."

"Yeah," he said.

"And you know so much more about them than anyone I know."

"What idea you done come up with now?"

"We can open up a motorcycle shop!"

I waved my tattered piece of notebook paper in the air. I was excited. I'd been up all night, planning and plotting and coming up with every little detail.

"You see this?" I said, pointing to my awful motorcycle figure. "We can call it Bike Nights. And I think you'll be happier. You can sell used motorcycle gear and—"

"And I can sell modification parts and lights and then they can sit down and drink a beer and—" He lit up. "Yeah. We could schedule bike rides on the weekends and Bike Nights would be the meet up spot."

"And I can take care of the business side."

We sat down at the table with oil-stained notebook paper scattered everywhere, listening to music. He'd drawn out the logo, while I searched for pricing for a place.

"Do you really think I can do it?" Kimani said.

"Yeah! You are one of the smartest people I know. Of course you can!"

"Yeah, but remember what happened last time?"

I laughed. "Yeah. I guess we are a little bit crazy."

I had just had Armani when I heard on a commercial, *"Missy Elliot is looking for new rappers. She is looking for the next big star."*

"Missy Elliot!" I yelled. I jumped up and ran into the bedroom.

"Bae," I said, beaming with a smile. "Bae, bae, bae."

He glanced away from his video game and looked at me. "What's up?"

"Missy Elliot got this contest and I think you can win. It's a rap contest."

"For real?" he said.

"Yeah! You can take a couple of days off and go and I bet you'll win. You're that damn good."

"Naw. I don't think I could win."

"You can," I said, jumping in place.

He went to work and asked his boss if he could take off the days. He needed three days to catch the bus from Cleveland, Ohio to Washington, DC.

"They ain't letting me take off, babe. It's cool. I'll get another opportunity."

"No! This *is* your opportunity. You have to take it!"

"Baby. I will lose my job."

"I don't care! We'll be all right."

Kimani didn't show up to work that weekend; he was on his way to DC instead. He came back a few days later, looking so defeated, I couldn't help but feel bad.

"I lost my job, I didn't win, and we gotta pay rent."

"What happened?" I asked.

"I made it through the rap round, but then they wanted me to sing." He looked at me and shook his head. "You know I can't sing."

"So, what you do?"

"I thought I might be able to get away with it by singing some R-Kelly, 'cause you know he don't really be blowing like that."

"And?"

"And they cut my ass and sent me home."

I wanted to laugh, but the bills wouldn't allow me a comical moment. Armani a newborn and he had no job, but as always, he found a way.

"I don't care, babe," I said. "We made it through. So, yes, I do believe you can do it."

"That's why I love you. No matter what, you always believed in me."

The next morning, I called and scheduled an appointment with the realtor, while he priced inventory, and our plan was coming into full effect. I saw a part of him that had been missing for so long. He smiled again.

CHAPTER TWENTY EIGHT

I had everything. I had two healthy girls, a husband who would die for me, and a stable job, yet it was still so hard to smile. I felt like I had been running all my life, chasing this picture-perfect life, yet when I finally got it all, I realized I had been running from something much deeper—and I couldn't run anymore. I couldn't blame him anymore. We had lived in our new beautiful house for a couple of months, yet every time I stepped onto the porch, I felt as if every ounce of me had been stripped away.

I tried playing it off, smiling when I was supposed to smile. I laughed even when I didn't think anything was funny, yet deep down inside, I was screaming for help. Something was chasing me, haunting me.

I concealed it.

The girls were with my mother, so I couldn't put the blame on them.

My husband was being so good to me, I could not use him as a scapegoat.

I prayed. I held my head up and I kept running.

But one night, it caught up with me.

"Babe. Something about this house is creepy. Like it's haunted or something," I said.

I laid down on Kimani's lap, while he played Call of Duty. I closed my eyes. He kissed my lips. "I know," he said. "I ain't wanna say nothing, but I hate being here by myself. The walls be making noises; I can hear things from upstairs. Something ain't right."

I laughed. "Momma told me to put some blessed oil on the walls."

"Well, did you?"

"Heck yeah!"

We let out a laugh so deep from within, it felt foreign. We were enjoying ourselves. No kids, just the two of us again. Our laugh eased into us gazing into each other's eyes. The lights flashed from the TV screen as he put the controller down onto the floor. He leaned in. He kissed me again. I turned away.

I sat up from his lap.

"What's wrong?"

"I heard something," I said. I pulled the curtain and peeked out the window.

It was almost midnight and the only thing I could see was the streetlights beaming on the cars and a man limping down the street with a ladder across his back.

"What is it?"

"Just a crackhead on his way to the scrap yard."

"What?"

We laughed again; then I sighed.

I couldn't help but stare at the house across the street. It was my grandmother's house, the home I'd spent my teenage years in. I had been so excited to know I was going to live on the same street I grew up on.

I closed the curtain and closed my eyes. The memories made my stomach churn as I slouched back down onto the couch.

"You okay?" He asked.

"Yeah."

"So, baby, the kids are gone. You know what that mean?" He said, winking an eye.

I nodded my head, but he could tell I wasn't really excited. Sex wasn't on my mind. It never really was. Most of the time, it hurt like hell. I couldn't understand for the life of me why women would be screaming, moaning, and begging for more. I must have missed something. The only pleasure I got from it was pleasing him, making him feel good. I did it because that was how I learned to make a man happy. That is, until I met Kimani. But even he had his needs.

"Sure," I said, nonchalantly. He could tell by the expression on my face that I was not feeling it. I was full of chicken wings and potato chips and ready to go to bed. I felt disappointed in myself. "I killed the vibe, didn't I?"

"Khadija, we only had sex once since the kids been gone and what was that, a month ago?"

"I know. I just haven't been feeling well," I said, with a slight smirk.

He looked at me and nodded his head. He knew I was just making up an excuse, like I always did. It was either a headache, my super-long period, or exhaustion from work. He had heard it all and I felt guilty. I felt horrible that I couldn't make him happy, especially since it was always his mission to make me smile.

I slouched deeper into the chair and listened. I listened to the little voice in my head chastising me, beating me down, and making me feel like nothing. *You suck. Why can't you just be normal? Can't even please your man. He's going to leave you. You're worthless. So many women would kill to have a man like yours. He does everything for you and look at you. Can't even satisfy him.*

I teared up but refused to let the tears fall. Instead, I put on a front like I had an attitude, smacking my lips, sighing deeply, and turning further away from him.

"I'll be back," he said. He stood up, snatched his coat from the door, and walked out.

And when he walked out, it felt like he wouldn't come back. And if he did, his love for me would be different.

I acted like I didn't care, but I did.

Get up and get your man, I thought. It seemed as if an angel was on my shoulder. *Tell him it's not his fault. Tell him he's a good man. Uplift that man. He's good enough.*

I couldn't do it. I glanced out the window and watched his brake lights illuminate the night. He paused at the stop sign for just a second, turned up his music to a deafening max, and then the only thing I could see was smoke from the tires as he peeled off.

You better do something. Save your marriage!

The voice was screaming at me. I thought about when I was a little kid, sitting in the back of the church, while my mother sat in the front row for a women's seminar. The kids were supposed to be coloring, our little ears too far to hear anything the grown women were talking about, but I'd heard it all.

The speaker, also a friend of my mother's, took off her robe. She stretched out her arms and she allowed the robe to fall onto the floor.

"Never deny your husband," she said. "The Bible says, 'Do not deprive one another.' Shut your mouth and give it up."

The women laughed and as a child, it was the most disgusting thing I'd ever heard an old woman say. But now, I was listening.

I ran upstairs and took a quick shower. I didn't have any lingerie, so I decided to go through his drawers to find one of his large white tees. I was getting excited. I was going to surprise him. I was going to make him happy.

I threw on my favorite song, "Overnight Celebrity," and then finished getting myself together by spreading some baby oil over my body.

I was glistening.

I showered myself with some Sweet Pea body spray.

It was on and popping.

He pulled up. The engine shut off and the music deadened. I got nervous. I wanted to cover up. I wanted to jump in the bed and act like I was asleep, just so he could be surprised I was naked.

Naw, Khadija, that's corny. Do a pose. Put one foot up on the couch and the other on the floor. And toot your booty out. He like that.

I laughed at myself, then rushed to mellow down the music and dim the lights.

As I waited for the door, my hands began to shake. He was my husband, but I was still nervous.

He walked in. He stopped to look at me. He dropped the bags to the floor and smiled. It was a million-dollar smile, and it brought me comfort. *He loves me.*

He took his hand, placed it on the arch of my back, and pulled me in for a kiss. As his lips drew into mine, nausea seemed to creep into my throat.

"I can't!" I yelled. I yanked back. "I can't do this!"

"What's wrong?"

I felt sickness rise from my stomach as my head began to spin. I swallowed it down, looked into his eyes, and then wiped his kiss from my lips in shame. I felt like trash, used-up and thrown away—nasty. I took a deep breath.

"Are you okay?"

"Yeah," I said, moving in closer.

I couldn't lose him. I had to keep going. I couldn't lose the very person who loved me, who would die for me. I pulled him closer to me. I kissed him, making sure he could feel the love and passion with each twist of my tongue. But no matter how hard I tried to close my eyes, lose myself, and forget, it wouldn't go away. I wanted to tell him.

I *needed* to tell him. I just couldn't.

I played it off as he touched my body, disguising my troubled heart.

Allowing him to continue made me feel as if I had not failed him after all. As his lips touched mine and his arm gripped my waist tighter, I began to drift off. My breathing grew quick. I was gone. My mind and my body were no longer there in that living room with Kimani. I was no longer twenty-two, or a strong-willed mother and wife.

I was fourteen.

It was hot and muggy in that dark attic just across the street. I could smell rotting cans of Budweiser; I could hear the fan spinning wildly in the windowsill and see that broken mirror. The mirror that had a hard crack zigzagging down the middle, yet still standing strong. The same mirror he'd bend me over in front of as he pleased himself.

I'd look in the mirror. I'd see a broken girl.

I'd look in the mirror. I'd see myself breaking apart, pieces of my innocence leaving me, scattered, too sharp to pick up and put back together.

My uncle. He was there. He smiled at me in that mirror. He adored me. He admired my body. He pulled back strands of my hair and whispered in my ear, "You are such an amazing girl."

Pulled into the present, I jumped back from Kimani. My hands shook. My body shivered, and tears streamed down my face. I was stuck. It hurt.

"Khadija!" Kimani yelled, as if he could see what I was seeing. "Baby," he said, grabbing me and wrapping his arms around me. "What's going on?"

"The smell," I whispered.

"What smell?" He said, pulling his shirt up to his nose. "I stink?"

"The beer. It's just strong. That's all."

He pulled away to examine me. It was as if I were physically broken somewhere and it was his job to find and fix it. "Why are you crying?"

"I don't know," I said.

I tried turning away, but he forced me to look back at him.

"I just need some time."

"Some time for what? You gon' sit down and tell me what's really going on. I know you. Did I do something?"

I looked up at him, feeling ashamed. He wouldn't understand. I could have stopped it. I'd let it happen, but when Kimani wiped my tears away, it seemed he'd wiped away my fears, too.

I lowered my head like a child who had done something horrible.

"My uncle molested me."

CHAPTER TWENTY NINE

It seemed the world had stopped.

Kimani had stopped breathing for sure. "What uncle?"

"My Uncle Trey."

"Your Uncle Trey? What the fuck? You talking about your uncle with the studio? The one I was about to record with?"

I nodded my head while wiping the tears from my chin.

"Get the fuck out of here! Ain't he like forty?"

He paced through the living room, as if he couldn't fathom what I'd said. He had anger in his eyes. He pointed to the house across the street. "That shit happened right there, Khadija! A couple of yards from where you lay your head at night?"

"Yeah."

"Why wouldn't you tell me?" He drew his fist up at the air, as if he wanted to hit something. "I can't believe we moved across the street from the very place you were abused. What the fuck?"

"We needed a place to stay," I said.

"Not *that* damn bad!" He snapped back. "We could have moved *anywhere*, Khadija. I don't care how big this house is. It ain't worth it. It just ain't worth it."

He stopped by the fireplace, placed his hand on the mantel, and then glanced at the picture of our two little girls. He grabbed his chest. "I don't know what I'd do if somebody touched my girls. God knows! I would kill them. What kind of man—Call your father. Call him right now and tell him what happened."

"What? No. I could never do that." My heart dropped deep into my stomach.

What if my father doesn't believe me? I thought. *What if he blames me?*

"But my father tried," I said. "He did. He wanted to know what was wrong with me. He just didn't know. He tried to make me happy."

"That ain't got shit to do with it. Stop making excuses and stand up for yourself. The shit happened, and everybody involved got to deal with it. You over here suffering, trying to save their fucking feelings, while they living all hunky-dory somewhere in La La Land. Fuck them."

There were times when Kimani was cool and calm, and then there were other times, when KG would come out. Now, KG was out and in full effect. Yet I still couldn't push myself to do it.

I thought about the days I sat in the car with my father as he drove me around the city. He would do a hundred circles around the same block, just waiting for me to talk to him. It didn't matter if he had just gotten off a ten-hour shift, or went from his first job to his second, remodeling someone's house or fixing up something; he would drive for hours in the dark, look straight ahead at the road until I told him what was wrong. My father did love me. But I still didn't know if this was too much to believe. *What would he think of me?*

"I can't do it."

"Yes, you can. And you will."

My eyes begged him to let it go, to not force me to do this, but his voice held no mercy. He handed me the phone, fingers over the numbers, and eyed me, urging me to get my shit together.

So many thoughts spun in my head as I gripped the phone. They were my uncle's words. They drowned all common sense. I was supposed to be loyal to him. "Men love loyal women," is what he'd say, and once again, it took me back. Once again, my memories took over and I was fourteen again, holding onto his every word. I believed him. I believed *in* him. He wasn't wrong. He was just trying to help a lost girl find herself.

His words rang deep inside and they were just as true as when he first looked into my eyes and said, "Khadija, you can't go around telling your friends about us. They'd get jealous and ruin it all. You don't want that, do you? Nobody would ever understand us. They wouldn't understand how beautiful you are. Your heart. You are special. No one really knows just how special you are, but me."

And that is when I remembered sitting on the porch with my best friend. It was the Nineties, when cars were still bumping Master P and kids rode their bikes up and down the streets, playing "Red Light, Green Light."

My heart raced, as I knew he'd caught me talking to her. I could see my uncle's shadow in the attic window. He'd heard me; he'd watched me as I poured my heart out to my best friend. I'd told her what happened and how it made me feel—Special, but that I was confused about it all and I wanted it to stop, but at the same time, I didn't. She shrugged me off, turned the boombox up, and we danced to Cam'ron's "Horse & Carriage," as if nothing had ever happened. She thought I was lucky. I could see it in her eyes. It was the first and last time I'd utter a word about it. Maybe she was right. It wasn't a big deal. He loved me, and he would love me like no other. I was special. And he reminded me of that every time he touched me. *How could I betray him?*

Plus, if he stopped treating me like a princess, then who would I have? Nobody. I couldn't dare go back to the days when I was treated like a child. He treated me like a Queen. Never talked down to me like I was not smart enough, like I was a teen. He treated me like I was equal, and he took me places. After a gig, we'd spend hours laughing, my high kicking in, feeling like no one in his world mattered but me.

He laughed at my corny jokes and he talked as if I was already great. He gave me books to read and drilled me about life. He was the first one to teach me about boys. Boys didn't deserve someone like me. I was much too loyal, intelligent, and focused. He bragged about me everywhere we went. He told everyone I was going to be great and everyone believed him, because he believed it, and therefore, I believed him, and what if I lost that? What if I lost the person who believed in me the most?

He trusted me, and I trusted him. He was right! They wouldn't understand. Why would someone who would make me read books and take me places and introduce me to people as if I were their child and —

"Khadija. If you don't call and tell your father, I will."

Kimani's stare hardened as I started to feel a bit threatened. But as I held that phone up to my chest, I knew that just telling my father would start to lighten the load on my heart.

"It wasn't right, Khadija."

The more he lectured me, the smaller I felt. My body shrunk at his words and I felt like a ten-year-old being scolded by their father. I held the phone in my hand, shaking, my heart racing so fast it seemed to beat through each vein in my body. I could barely catch my breath.

"Daddy," I said.

"What's up, Peanut?"

My heart sank even lower. He answered the phone with such cheer in his voice. He was happy to hear from me. I was his little girl again, even after all those years.

"He touched me," I said.

"Who touched you?" His voice shook, as if I'd torn his heart in two. He stuttered, and I could imagine the beads of sweat pouring from his hairline, his glasses fogging up, just like it did when I first told him I was ready to have sex. I didn't want to hurt him.

"Uncle Trey."

My heart beat fast over the silence.

"Let me call you back."

He hung up the phone and I waited. All kinds of things were going through my head.

What would I do if my uncle denied it? What would I say?

He called me back, each ring churning at my stomach. I wondered what my father had said to him.

I answered the phone but didn't say anything. I just listened to my father's faltering voice.

"He said he wanted me and you to sit down with him and talk. But he said he doesn't want your husband to be there."

"Fuck that!" Kimani yelled. "I don't give a fuck. I'm going to be there and I'm sitting right next to that pedophile ugly-ass looking—"

I muffled the phone, turning away. "Okay," I whispered. Then I hung up the phone. "I can't do this! I don't want to do this!"

"You *have* to do it," Kimani said. "You gotta live with that shit. He done gone on with his life and *you* the one gotta live with that shit every single day."

Two days later, we pulled up into my father's driveway. My eyes were swollen from crying and the sleepless nights had caused such lightheadedness, I felt too weak to walk.

"It's going to be okay," Kimani said. "I'm going to be right there by your side."

We walked into the backyard. My father was sitting there on the patio deck. My uncle sat in a chair next to him. He looked different to me. Much older, as if the alcohol had eaten him away, or maybe it was guilt. He looked afraid, surprised to see my husband by my side.

I grabbed my husband's hand. I gripped it tight, drawing strength from him. I walked to our seat, a wicker love seat with big, fluffy pillows on it.

I took a deep breath and sat down.

It was quiet for a second. No one knew where to start.

And then the most magical thing happened. I sat straight up in my chair, like a Queen finding her throne. I looked my uncle dead in his eyes as a great wave of strength shot through my body.

"How could you forget?" I yelled. "How could you forget what you did to me?"

My body shook a bit, but something was stirring up inside me. I no longer felt my husband's presence. He was not there. And my father wasn't there, either. It was just me, my uncle, and a surge of brave, yet gripping energy birthing from the depths of my spirit. I wasn't fourteen anymore.

"I don't really remember," he said. "I was on cocaine. I had a bad habit back then and I just don't remember everything."

I pulled away from Kimani's hand and leaned in so far, I almost fell out of my chair. "You don't remember sticking your dick in my mouth?"

It spilled from my guts—spoiled rotting words—a disease, finally purging from my body.

I focused on his every move. I didn't care anymore. I didn't care about being loyal. I didn't care about hurting anyones feelings; I needed to get it out. It was hurting me. It was killing me.

I needed to live.

"I remember what you tasted like. I can never forget it; how salty it was and how you said it was natural and that I was being a good girl to you. You knew what you were doing!"

Those words were so foreign to me. I'd never talked like that, especially in front of my father, but my spirit was doing the talking - it was healing.

"I know. I did it. I'm so sorry Khadija," he said.

I exhaled.

"You are right. You are absolutely right. I was wrong."

I glanced at my father to make sure he'd heard it.

I was not a bad child; I was not someone who was trying to tear apart the household, break up the family. I was only fourteen. I was confused. I was searching for something.

My husband gripped my hand so hard and stared at my uncle as if he was going to leap out his chair and kill him.

My father was so shocked, he stared at my uncle too.

And my uncle. He had this look on his face. One that only I could understand. It was as if he couldn't believe I had let him down. It wasn't a look of disappointment or hurt. He was telling me he had forgiven me for everything I'd said and was going to say. He forgave me for breaking our covenant, and he still loved me and would always love me. And when I looked into his eyes it didn't matter the coarse and graphic words that shot from my lungs; I knew my uncle would never understand. He would never see the extent of damage his manipulation had done to me, to my mind, my marriage, the way I looked at men, the way I raised my kids.

I closed my eyes as something just as deep, fought its way out. I felt like I was going crazy. I was confused. I'd done everything I was supposed to do. I stood up to him. I told him, but I didn't really want to be there. And my uncle was not the one I wanted to hurt. I looked at my father as a tear streamed down his face, and I realized, that tear made me feel better because it was my father who I wanted to hurt.

CHAPTER THIRTY

Even before the yelling, the screaming and dishes shattering downstairs, I knew I had done something really terrible.

I was only thirteen, but I just knew.

The birds were chirping that morning and the sun was shining beautifully through my grandmother's bedroom window. I was sleeping peacefully, tossing, turning and enjoying my grandmother's pillow top when I heard her.

"You did what, Damon?" She yelled. "You fucking did what?"

My eyes shot open. For a second, I had forgotten where I was.

Again, she screamed, "Damon!"

The rage in her voice scared me, yet I couldn't understand a word.

I didn't know if her slurred words were from drunkenness or my inability to wake up, but once she yelled my father's name, the way I'd never heard her say it before, it became clear she'd snapped.

"How could you do this to me?" She yelled.

It was my stepmother, and she was pissed.

"I can't believe you!"

I jumped out of the bed scared and confused. It definitely wasn't a dream. Then it dawned on me.

Last night. Oh. My God. It was me!

I felt sick to my stomach, like I had taken one too many trips at the Golden Corral buffet. My stomach had knotted up. I had to use the bathroom.

"KHADIJA!" My father yelled.

Yep, it definitely was me.

I was afraid to answer. I wanted to be a kid again. Preferably eight years old, too young to get a real whipping, not thirteen and a half.

Maybe I should play like I'm sleeping.

"Khadija! Come here!"

I tiptoed to the hallway, my back sliding along the wall. I took my time walking as light as possible, so I could ease my way into the chaos. I got to the landing, dipped my head out just enough to hear them clearer and then it happened. She read it, word for word. My language, my letter.

I can't stand that we are always over Miss. P house. Why do we always have to go to her house just to watch movies, why can't we just go to the movies, just me and my dad?

The words shot fear through me and the more she read it, the more I had to boo boo. It was becoming too real the extent of my problems; and it was just getting started.

I bravely walked down one step at a time, each step bringing me closer to my demise. Each step causing my heart to beat even faster; like a car revving, waiting to speed off into the distance. I pulled myself together. I was almost there. One step and I was in the living room. Another step, I was in hell.

There was broken glass on the kitchen floor, an empty bottle of vodka and horns had grown straight out of my stepmother's head. She was red in color and out of her mind.

My father stood in the living room with his hands resting on top of his head, looking helpless, homeless and confused. He was thrown off of his game. *What could he say?* He'd been ratted on, he'd been exposed, and there was nothing he could do about it. He couldn't deny the words that she had read over and over again in that letter. He looked stunned. He was speechless, and when he saw me, his disappointment in me broke my heart.

I tried to let him know that it was an honest mistake, that I would never be disloyal to him. I loved him, and we were best friends. Best friends didn't tell secrets. I would never try to hurt him. But he didn't understand. He could no longer read my language and he no longer cared to understand me. He looked at me as if he couldn't even recognize the little girl who once stole his heart.

I was just as confused as he was. I honestly didn't know how I had left that piece of paper on the table. I thought I had taken it upstairs with my notebook. I must have been exhausted, tired. My eyes were puffy from crying so much. I don't know, maybe I couldn't see. Maybe I was distracted.

Don't be mad at me daddy. I swear I didn't do it on purpose.

In my mind, I begged for his approval, his love, but it wasn't there. I could see it in his eyes. Just like that, he hated me. I needed him to hug me, to comfort me, but when I reached out to him, he turned his back on me.

It hurt like never before.

I studied my father as he walked out of the house, frustrated and in deep thought, strategizing his next move. My stepmother had stormed out, still talking gibberish and I was left alone with my grandmother. Everyone in the house looked at me as if I were a huge problem, a home wrecker. I was no longer a good child, someone worth investing their love in. To them, I possessed an evil, conniving spirit.

Why would I do that on purpose? I thought. *I love my father. Yes, I did say that I wanted them to separate, but suddenly I have a change of heart. I didn't mean it. I just want them to be happy. I would do anything to take it back.*

I listened to KCI and JoJo's " All My Life " to numb the pain. I wanted to completely block out all of my feelings and forget it ever happened, but the words just kept hitting too close to home.

All my life I only wanted to live with my father. I only wanted to spend time with him. I messed it up. I knew it. He'd bought me that very album just a few months earlier. It was something I could never forget. It was the morning of my birthday, and he played the song until I woke up. When I heard the song, I jumped out of bed and ran down the steps and there he was. He stood with a huge smile right next to a brand new boom box with my favorite song playing. He always knew what would make me happy, but those moments were gone. Listening to the song only made me feel worse.

I thought about writing. Writing always made me feel better. I picked up my notebook. I threw it back down. My writing seemed to always get me into trouble.

I let a couple of days pass before trying to talk to my dad. I waited as long as I could.

"Hey dad," I said, trying to act cool as if he could have magically forgotten. "Dad?"

He didn't respond, he just looked at me. He pointed to the letter that I had written and said. "So, you mean to tell me that you didn't intend to write this and leave it out for Erica to see?"

I shook my head, trying to get him to see that I would never do that.

His voice got louder, his disappointment more intense, "Come on Khadija! You are too smart for this!"

He threw the paper up in the air and walked out.

I picked up the ruffled paper, regretting ever picking up the pen to write in the first place. I studied it. It had been crumbled and flattened out numerous times, and some of the ink bled past the pink margins. It was just like me, worthless.

I smoothed the paper against my palm and my thigh. I looked at the letter and began to read the words that had changed my life. As I began reading it, it was like someone else had written it. I had to second guess myself because I could barely recognize even its handwriting. I mumbled the words:

I hate her. I wish she would just go away. I can't stand that we are always over Miss. P house. Why do we always have to go to her house just to watch movies, why can't we just go to the movies, just me and my dad?

Oh, I forgot, we do go to the fucking movies. But guess who the fuck shows up. That big booty bitch. I can't stand her. She is always around. She even came to North Carolina with my dad. She went to the beach with us; she ate dinner with us, she did everything with us. He didn't come to see me. He's a fucking liar. He came to be with her. I hate her. I hate her. I hate her. Disappear, just fucking disappear.

Well. I guess I did write it. But, I couldn't connect with the person that wrote it. It was like a spirit that was inside of me jumped from my body to the paper, and the lines in the paper held the demonic words captive. That person was angry. I'm not angry. That person seemed distraught. Man, I'm cool - at least I wanted to be. All I wanted to do was fix it. I wanted my father's love back, and there was only one person who could help me. I had to pick up the phone. I had to call her.

CHAPTER THIRTY ONE

The next day my father barely talked to me. My stepmother was mad at me, and everyone in the house thought that I was not to be trusted.

I had never felt so lonely in my life. I would lay in the bed and think about my mother, my brothers, and sisters that I had dipped out on and daydream about the last time I saw them. It was the only thing that brought me comfort. I imagined my mother was praying for me.

I was always breaking a family apart. Everyone was right. I was a horrible person. How could my mother ever forgive me for how I betrayed her? How could my father?

Again, I was spiraling into a depression, suicidal thoughts consuming my mind. I started to feel like it was better than having to face my reality. *No one loves me.*

More days went by, and things didn't change.

"Hi, dad, where are you going?" I'd ask my dad.

I couldn't wait to see him leaving so I could have an excuse to talk to him.

"Out."

"Oh, can I go?"

"Did you do your homework and your chores?"

I stared at the floor. I knew what he really meant. I turned around and walked back upstairs. No need to debate, it was useless. It was a done deal. No more trips with dad. No more smiles when he saw me. *I might as well replace my halo with the devil's horn and walk around with a pitchfork because that is all I would ever be in his eyes.*

As I heard the front door close, I ran towards his bedroom window. I had a great view of him. I watched him get into the car, extend his arm to the radio, turn it up and throw the car into reverse. He had left me.

I wanted him to call me Peanut. I wanted to be his sidekick again. *I could be trusted. I would never, ever say anything again.*

There was one more thing I could do, I thought. *I should pick up the phone and see if she could help.*

I ran downstairs to call her - the only other person who seemed to care about me. *But she is in that letter.* I had ratted her out too. But I missed her. I missed her taking me places and taking me shopping and making me feel really pretty.

Maybe she is mad at me. Or maybe she forgave me. Call her Khadija. No. You can't. But you must!

I picked up the phone and dialed the number. I swallowed deeply and tried controlling the fear in my voice.

"Miss P," I said, as soon as she picked up.

"Yes," she said.

Yes, I thought. *Finally, someone cared.*

"Um. I wanted to know if you still had my dress for my eighth-grade prom and —

There was silence.

"Miss P, you there?"

She still didn't say anything. It was as if she was thinking of what to say. I could hear her breathing.

"Hello?"

"You got the nerve to call me about a damn dress! What?"

I couldn't speak. I couldn't even find the words to say.

"No. You're not getting that dress. I took it back. And you know what? What you did was wrong."

"I'm sorry! I really didn't —

She interrupted me. "If it wasn't for me telling your father to keep you, he would have sent you back! But no, I told your father to give you another chance."

I swallowed deeply. I couldn't believe what she had said. I wanted to cry. I wanted to scream. I wanted to pick up a knife and just kill myself once and for all. My father hated me.

I couldn't fathom my father not wanting me. As much as I had done to my mom, she always wanted me.

"Khadija, what are you doing over there on the floor?" my Uncle Trey said, peeking his head through the doorway.

"Nothing. Um. Just picking up. Um." I looked around to see what I could pretend to be picking off the carpet, but there was nothing there.

"Come on up here and talk to me."

"Who me?" I pointed to my chest.

He laughed. "Yes, you. Who else would I be talking to?"

I followed him to the attic. It smelled like lavender incense and baby powder up there. The futon was nicely decorated with pillows, and there was a tall broken mirror against the wall. The small window on the side allowed minimal fresh lighting, so it was kind of dark, but he had one light bulb shining brightly above his studio equipment that gave it just enough life.

I looked at my Uncle. He wore light blue jeans, a black button down, and a tie. He'd just came home from a gig. He knelt down on the floor and grabbed his guitar. He looked at me. He hummed some words. He smiled.

He glanced down at the strings as he made them dance and then he looked me dead in my eyes. He let me know he was ready to listen.

"So, what's wrong with you? You over there looking like a sad puppy who lost her way."

"What's wrong with me?" I shouted, "Everyone in this house hates me."

He laughed.

"No one hates you. They are just trying to figure things out. You threw a grenade up in here."

He laughed. "They are just trying to pick up the pieces."

"But, I really didn't mean to do it, Uncle Trey."

"I know."

"You know?"

"I know my niece, and I know that you would never try to hurt your father. You worship the ground he walks on. I wish I had a daughter that loved me like that. I have three sons, and I love them to death, but they are boys. They are not worried about me; they are into their own thing."

"No one believes me. Everyone thinks that I did it on purpose, that I am bad."

"Hold up. Hold up. Stop it. First of all, you need to stop worrying about what people think. Second, who fucking cares how your father feels about the situation. That's his problem, not yours. He did that, not you."

Those words alone freed me. I was able to let it go and stop worrying.

For the next couple of hours, I talked, and he listened. He answered every single question I had about life and we talked about things that I'd always wanted to say to an adult. And he didn't treat me like a kid. He didn't treat me as if I was beneath him and when I didn't understand, he was patient. Instead of talking down on me or giving up, he explained it until I could understand. Before I knew it, I had a thirst for more of his wisdom. I craved to read the books he read, learn about history and anything else he wanted to teach me.

"Can I hang out with you, Uncle Trey?" I asked.

"Anytime," he said.

I pulled away from that moment, stood up and walked back into the house. I was met with my teary eyed stepmother who held me tight and whispered how sorry she was. How it had happened to her and that if she would have known she would have done something. I needed to hear those words. I needed to hear that it wasn't my fault and that she believed me and that she was sorry.

She invited us over for Sunday dinner the next day, and it felt good to say 'yes.'

I had wasted a lot of years being bitter and mad at everyone, and I was finally ready to start over. Forgiveness felt good. It healed me. I'd found my pain, faced it and birthed a new outlook on life. Yet and still, it was not over. Little did I know, facing my uncle and dealing with the pain of things I kept hidden inside was a walk in the park compared to what I would face next.

CHAPTER THIRTY TWO

A couple of days later we made our way back to my father's house.
"You alright," he kept asking.

"Yes," I kept saying.

The truth is, it was awkward being around him. I was an adult, twenty-years-old, yet a couple of days ago, I felt like a lost thirteen-year-old needing her father.

"You sure you are all right?"

I stood by the grill and stared into the rack of chicken wings as they curled up under the fire.

"Yes, dad," I said.

I didn't say much else. We barely talked, but I had a ton of things going through my mind. I wanted to tell him that I had forgiven him, that I had started writing again. I longed to just to sit down with him and have another heart to heart about life; how I had found out just how young he was when he had me, only sixteen. He was in his twenties when he came to my rescue in North Carolina. He was even younger than that when he picked me up every summer to teach me how to craft wood, build relationships with key community leaders and how to go after whatever I wanted as if my life depended on it.

"I love you, dad," I said.

"I love you, too."

I also wrote about my mother. I missed her a lot, and after looking back over her life, many questions started burning inside. I had a feeling something terrible had happened to her. The way she raised us. It was as if she was running away from something and didn't want us to experience it.

I sat back down with Kimani, blocking the sun from my face. I moved under his arm and rested my head on his shoulder.

"Babe," I said. "I feel really good. Free."

He looked at me as the barbecue smoke blew over into our conversation. He smiled. "I know."

"All of these years I thought I was getting back at everyone for doing me wrong, not talking to people and just being mean, but really, all this time I wasn't hurting them. It was just killing me."

"It's crazy, huh?"

"Real crazy. I need to see my mom. I need to talk to her. I have been thinking about her a lot lately and having some weird crazy dreams. Remember the one I had of her in the casket?"

"Yeah."

"I'm still having them. I just need to talk to her and ask her some questions."

He held my hand as if he admired my strength. "We'll be there next week to pick up the kids. I think it would be really good for you to talk to her."

"I know. I just feel so bad."

He placed his finger up under my chin and pulled me in. He kissed my forehead and whispered, "You are always putting the world on your shoulders. You can't fix everything."

"I know, but I didn't call her back. She told me to call her back, but I forgot."

He handed me the phone. "Call her now."

"She is going to be so mad at me. I always forget to call her back."

I opened the phone.

It started ringing.

I laughed.

"Babe. Guess what?" I wore a huge smile on my face. It was a breath of fresh air.

"What?"

"It's my mom."

I smiled so hard, knowing my mother was always thinking about me. No matter how bad I treated her, she always loved me and wanted to make sure I was okay. She always had this strong intuition. I couldn't wait to hear her voice.

I walked into my father's house running from the loud music playing in the backyard.

The phone rang again.

I stepped into the kitchen and looked at her number. I took a deep breath.

The phone rang once more.

I answered it. "Ma! I am so sorry I forgot —-"

"This is Malika," a voice said.

I looked at the number and then paused.

"Dee," she said. "You hear me? This is Malika. Your mother is dead. She is in the ambulance. They are trying to resuscitate her."

The phone dropped from my hand as my knees crashed to the floor. My body went numb. I forgot where I was. Her words snatched the breath straight out of my body. I'd lost my mind.

"No!" I screamed, throwing my hands up as if surrendering to God.

I begged. I pleaded. "God please help me!"

Kimani ran into the kitchen, the screen door slamming into the frame. "Khadija! Something wrong with the kids!" he said.

"No!" I bawled. "I can't take this!"

I shook my head. I grabbed my chest. I screamed.

"What?" Kimani yelled.

"My mother is dead!"

"What?"

"My mother is dead!" I cried. "What am I going to do!"

"Get up!" Kimani said, pulling at me. "Get up right now!"

He didn't give me a chance to think. He just kept pulling at me. I could barely see him through my teary eyes, and I didn't have the strength to stand up. He picked me up off the floor.

"Where we going?" I said, trying to understand his words.

"We're going to go see your mom."

"But we don't have any money."

"I don't care. Let's go!"

My father snatched his credit card out of his wallet and placed it in Kimani's hand. We jumped into our Ford Expedition, grabbed some mattress money and a book bag and was on the road within thirty minutes.

I couldn't control my breathing. I tried not to think about it. Her last words, "Call me back when the movie is over."

"But she loved me!" I yelled. "I let her down. I always let her down."

Suddenly, I could remember every little thing my mother did for me.

"Pat a cake. Pat a cake. Bakers man." It was the last moment I remembered spending with her. I closed my eyes and allowed the darkness of the night to consume me. I remembered her smile as she bounced my baby on her lap. She tapped my babies little feet, kissed her little hands and smiled so big, it seemed she was having the time of her life. She sang to my nine-month-old. "Roll it up and put it in the pan."

She laughed.

Chapter Thirty Three

The Intensive Care Unit was full of mourning mothers, fathers and sisters and brothers. The place was consumed with stillness as I walked past still bodies barely clinging on to life. The family members walked the halls like the walking dead, and I wondered just how long it would take for me to turn, to lose myself. It took exactly ten steps, a glance at my mother lying still on the bed with a busted lip, tape strapping down the plastic tubing cut deep into her throat.

"Mommy!" I yelled. I broke down.

I couldn't remember the last time I'd called her that. The last time I felt like I needed to be in her arms.

I examined every machine hooked up to her body and listened to the sounds giving her life. They were harsh sounds, beeping and pushing and pumping, but I was thankful for them.

I couldn't believe it was my mother lying there. The very one who had raised me. She sacrificed so much for me, for my brothers and sisters and for anyone who needed her. She was just alive, talking to me. And all she wanted was for me to pick up the phone and call her back.

My brother held on to me. His body shivered at bit, yet he stood strong.

I pressed forward. "God! Please give me one more chance to tell my mother I understand. You weren't trying to hurt me, ma. You were trying to make sure I didn't get hurt like you. I know you were hurting, ma. I'm so sorry!"

I knelt down to her, her eyes running with tears. I held her hand tight. "You were trying to protect me!"

She laid there as if she could not hear a word. She was still. I'd never seen her so still in my life.

I talked to her for hours, but it seemed, I was talking to myself. The doctors would come and go, sometimes saying a few words, while other times writing notes and then walking back out. Most of the time they'd come in to remind us of her condition, to recommend in the most callous way that she had no chance. We reminded them of the God we served.

We spent our nights stretched out in the ICU waiting room, with thin covers that exposed the bottom half of our dingy looking clothes. We woke up before the morning nurses came in, snuck into the bathroom with a hospital toothbrush and tube of toothpaste and used some extra towels from my mom's room to wash up. We had no money. We had no place to stay, and our kids were with my mother's friend.

Weeks went by and still no change in her condition.

Another week passed and we finally got kicked off the ICU floor. We then slept in our car for a day before my childhood church gave my brother money to get us all a motel room. We were desperate, all ten of us. It was me, Kimani, my brother, his wife, my sister and a half dozen of my aunts and my grandmother all cramped up in a motel room. We didn't care. As long as we could walk across the parking lot to hold my mother's hand, it didn't matter where we laid our head.

The motel lasted about a week before finally we had to find jobs and a place to stay. Kimani moved our things from Cleveland to North Carolina, found us a place and started working. We were not going to leave my mother, and Kimani was there to make sure of it.

Through it all, my mother was still in a coma. All we could do was wait and flag down a doctor when we could. And although they would always come back with worse news, there was something about seeing them that gave us hope that their next visit would be different.

One morning it was. I sat with my mother and talked to her. I rubbed her hand and kissed her forehead when a school of doctors marched into my mother's room. Some looked as if they had been up all night, while others were overly anxious to see a comatose patient. I stepped to the side.

"Dorothy, can you hear me?" the doctor said.

He didn't give her a chance to respond.

"This is Dorothy," he said to the students. "She is a 47-year-old female suffering from a massive heart attack. Due to aphasia, she has no brain activity. We implanted a stint, and she has undergone a blood transfusion. She has a ten percent chance of surviving. If she survives, she will do so in a vegetation state."

I eyed the doctors. "What the hell?"

The words they were speaking were so vile, they seemed to curse her.

"I'm sorry. I didn't realize you were here."

"Excuse me," my brother said, barging into the room. He nudged his way pass the doctors. "I need some time with my mother?" He eyed the doctors and then commanded the crew to exit by pointing to the path directly out the door.

The heart monitor sped up. It beat stronger and stronger, the numbers going higher by the second.

She wasn't moving, but I could feel that she could hear the authority in my brother's voice. It was something about his energy.

"All right, Momma," my brother said. "Time for you to get up and out that bed, now. You've been sleeping for far too long! Time to get up!"

He walked up to her bed and stared at her. "Mom. Get up!"

He was so sure she was going to wake up, it made me nervous. *Was he going crazy?*

I looked up at my brother. He seemed a lot stronger than a few weeks before. He was always strong, a muscular build and athletic stature, but on this day, he moved differently.

He swung a duffel bag off his shoulders and onto the nightstand. He didn't even look my way. He focused on my mother.

Beep. Beep. Beep.

The heart monitor jumped again.

"What are you doing?" I asked. "I don't think she can hear you."

He slowly turned toward me. He grinned. "Yes, she can. She can hear everything we are saying."

He forced the bag open as if he was about to perform surgery. "You are about to get out of this bed, ma. One way or the other. Let's get to work!"

My eldest sister then marched in. "Ma. You ready to get up so we can start our day? It's morning."

She threw the curtain back and allowed the sunlight to rain down on my mother's body. "You know you'd be out this bed cleaning the house by now. Stop acting all tired. Get up!"

I looked at my mother who laid there as if not even a chainsaw could wake her. I glanced back at my brother, my sister, then back at my mother.

Did they know something I didn't know?

My brother reached into his backpack and pulled out some headphones. He slid them onto her ear and then pressed down on the cassette player. It was the Mississippi Mass Choir singing, "Having You There." Their voices burst through the headphones bringing church right into the ICU room. They praised God, they sang, they beat on the tambourines and my spirit was lifted so high, something in me just wanted to praise God too.

"You know that's your favorite song," my brother said. "You gonna help them sing it? You know you miss singing in the choir."

My sister took a damp cloth and wiped the blood from my mother's cracked lips. She sang too and talked to my mother as if they were carrying a conversation.

"You gone be late for church. Everybody out here asking where Sis. Williams is. What you want me to tell them? You too tired to get up? You done lost your faith? Is that what you want me to tell them?"

"Faith the size of a mustard seed," I whispered.

My sister looked at me and smiled. She then kept wiping my mother's face, massaging it and speaking life into her. She picked my mother's eye boogers out her eyes and massaged baby lotion deep into her hands and feet, all the while keeping her eyes locked in on my mother.

I left the room. I couldn't take it anymore. The energy was overwhelming, and it stirred something inside of me. I felt strange. It was as if they were actors in a play. They were walking around talking and acting as if my mother could hear them.

"You okay?" My husband asked.

"Yeah," I said. He hugged me. "Your mother is going to be alright."

"I know my mother is going to be just fine," I said.

My husband pulled away from me. "What you say?"

I couldn't believe it either. My thoughts were changing, my words were changing, and I even felt a little different. I had all of this energy surging inside of me, and I didn't know what to do with it. I needed to write.

So many good memories were flooding my thoughts. All I could think about was the good times - the times my mother actually smiled. The day I won the spelling bee, the days she'd take us to the beach and how proud she was when we'd gotten honor roll or perfect attendance.

I wrote that night and then that morning. I wrote until I was exhausted and couldn't think another thought. I visited her the next day. I was excited. I couldn't wait to reminisce with her.

"Do you remember when Junior put dishwashing liquid in grandma's fish tank? Suds poured out like a broken foam machine, and the fish grandma had for years were floating upside down in Palmolive. Soap spilled all over the floor." I laughed. "And the look on your face!"

"You remember that?"

I laughed, then stopped. I got sad. My mother couldn't laugh with me.

I pulled out my letter, unfolding it carefully as to respect the stillness of the room.

"Ma. I'm going to read you something." I scooted my chair closer to her bed. "I really want you to listen."

I took a deep breath. I cleared my throat. I glanced at my mother. "Here goes."

I sighed.

Dear mom,

All I could ever remember was seeing you at the kitchen table with piles of bills mounted up everywhere. Bills from months ago, bills with cut off notices and then the ones you threw in the trash because you knew you couldn't pay them.

I remember you were always worried about money. You cried a lot, but you prayed more. You had so much faith, mom. And your bible was so big, I remember you asked me to bring it to you one day and I almost broke my little back. You had birthdates in there, death dates and Polaroids of each one of your children. You were so proud of us.

You didn't have a lot of money, mom, but what you did have, you used to the fullest. You took us to the library each week so we could fall in love with reading like you. You made sure we got to church, and on time, even though sometimes we didn't have a car. You made us walk a mile to get that word. We never missed a day of school even if we were bleeding half to death. And you gave us faith. No matter what, we never went hungry, we always had a roof over our heads, and you always showed us how much you loved us.

I glanced up at the ceiling to work through my tears. I glanced back at my mother. I let the tear fall. I wiped it, then gently kissed her cheek.

And even though I never told you this, I am so grateful you made me wear those old-fashioned, ugly dresses from the thrift store. You made me feel uncomfortable showing my body. While other girls had their stomachs out and wore tight pants showing their shape, I kept it classy. While everyone else was worrying about name brands, I saved my money and just shopped for what I liked. I stood out. I hated being the outcast in elementary school and middle, but when I got older, being different saved me. I was able to snatch up a good man, ma, because I stood out. Kimani saw something different in me. And even though he didn't know it and neither did I, it was because you raised me differently.

I'm sorry for taking you for granted, ma. For saying I hated you and for never showing you just how much you mean to me. But today I sit here with you, and I realize something. Ma, I never hated you. I only hated myself. I hated myself all of those years because I loved you so much. It hurt me to the core seeing you struggle every day to put food on the table. It hurt seeing him hurt you and I wasn't strong enough to stop him. I felt weak, angry, and I just wanted to run away from that feeling of being powerless.

Seeing you here has changed me, ma. I feel so much stronger, mom. I am no longer helpless. I have dreams. Big dreams and once you wake up, I'm going to show you a life you could never imagine. That's a promise. On my life, mom. On my life. I will make you proud.

Your daughter,

Khadija

CHAPTER THIRTY FOUR

Every day after, I carried around a notebook. I was determined. I would keep my promise. The thick five subject notebook was my diary. I wrote about things that hurt me, people, who helped me and every lesson I could think of. I jotted the funny moments, the hurtful ones, but most importantly, my dreams.

My dreams. I had no idea what I wanted to do with my life, so I'd ask myself questions in the notebook.

What do you love to do?

I don't know.

What did you love to do?

When I was seven, I wanted to be an actress. I wanted to be a veterinarian, but don't love animals enough. I love psychology because of my uncle. I wanted to own a business, just like my dad. I wanted to go into the military, just like my stepfather. I loved the structure, discipline and how proud he was serving the country.

"Babe," I said, while eating a sandwich. "I don't know what I want to be."

"Be a writer?"

I smacked my lips. "Yeah. Right!"

"No seriously. You remember those stories you used to send me in Iraq?"

I laughed. "They were so corny, Kimani."

"No. Actually, they weren't."

I shrugged it off and began to write down more things I used to like, but nothing stuck. Nothing gave me that energy I was looking for, until one night, I woke up from a nightmare.

The dream paralyzed me for a second. It was hard for me to move. It was difficult to speak. The words I tried to yell, trying to get Kimani to wake me up, came out as faint whispers.

The man in my dream just wouldn't stop whipping the little boy. The woman just wouldn't stop yelling, screaming and telling the man to stop.

Kimani shook me. "Babe. Babe. Wake up."

I cried in my sleep, my body stiff and numb. *I can't move. I can't wake up.*

"Babe," he said. He rubbed my arm. He gripped my hand. "Wake up. Wake up." He said. "You having another nightmare."

I fought my way out of the dream, but couldn't escape the room where it was happening. She was beating at the door. She was begging for him to stop. I could hear the door click closed, my brother's cry for help. I was little, just eight years old, but I could imagine what was happening behind that door. I could relate it to Kunta Kinte yelling as each whip tore flesh from his back. I could imagine my stepfather's strong hands holding him up, with suds dripping down his leg as he snatched another piece of skin from his backside.

"Get up. Get up and write," Kimani said. "That's the only way. That's the only way you are going to stop having nightmares."

I could hear Kimani in my dream as I heard my brother's cry.

"Go write," he whispered.

I whipped the cover from over my body and jumped out of the bed. I snatched my laptop from my desk and ran into the closet. I sat down on top of a heap of clothes, a heel sticking me in my back, and I wrote. I didn't care what I wrote or how it came out; it just felt so magical writing. I refused to lose that dream. I would step out of that room until I wrote down every single detail of what happened in that world.

I cried through the scene. My fingers shook as I wrote in that cramped, dark space. I loved it. I loved the adrenaline, the rush of getting the words down as fast as my mind could register them. I felt David's sadness, his defeat, because I was once there. I understood how it felt to feel helpless as a mother and want so badly to do something about your situation, because I was there. It was just a different form, and I dug for that reality. I reached deep inside and connected with my own fears, doubts and straight determination in order to write as if I myself, lived every moment of the scene. *What was I feeling when I was eight-years-old? What was I thinking?* That eight-year-old girl thought that if she could make him go away somehow, she would. But she was much too young, much too powerless, but she could do something else.

As I was writing, I thought about what I did to get back at him, to help myself, my eight-year-old mind settle down at night.

I waited until he went to sleep. I washed up and got ready for bed just like my mother had told me. I wore a long cotton gown with Sebastian and the little mermaid floundering through the sea. I looked to my left. I looked to my right as I gripped the frame of the doorway. It was dark. Everyone was sleep. The house was quiet. I tiptoed to the bathroom, locked the door, ran the water so no one would hear me and I searched for my stepfather's toothbrush. *Was his toothbrush the grey one with the thick beat up bristles or was it the one that stood up firm and tall?* I thought about it. It was definitely the thick beat up one. I pulled the toothbrush from the holder and lifted the toilet seat. I took the brush and scrubbed the darkest parts of the toilet, ran water over it and put it back. It felt good. I was no longer a helpless victim. I could get back at him. I could do something to make him pay. And as he hummed over the sink the next morning, brushing his teeth, paste bubbling from his mouth, I smiled. I smiled so hard, and my heart filled up with so much joy I could not hide it.

"What's wrong," my stepfather asked. He glanced at me, pausing the stroke of the brush.

"Nothing, dad."

"You sure. You're just sitting there in the hallway, watching me brush my teeth. Huh?"

"Yep."

I got up, ran into the living room and grabbed the second remote, Luigi, from Mario Brothers. I sat there silent, with my brother by my side as he stared into Mario's world. I scooted over to get as close to him as possible. *Everything is going to be alright*, I thought. *I got him back.*

I laughed out loud in that little dark closet, thinking about being eight again, and then I wiped the tears from my eyes as I finished my last sentence. It was one of the most difficult things for me to write, but it was necessary. I wasn't writing it for it to become a book. I didn't care about who was going to read it or what they were going to say. I sat in the dark closet, with myself and my world and I danced in it, I lived in it, and it was the closest I ever felt to being myself.

The closet was my safe space, a space where I didn't have to apologize for being me. I could say what was on my mind. I could be myself without judgement. I could tell my truths, and it felt good to finally be able to use my voice - to finally feel like I was good enough in this world just the way I was.

I stood up, drained of every ounce of energy I had. I slid back into the bed with my husband. He turned, held me and asked me if I was okay.

"Yes," I said.

Hours later, I would jump back up. I would run into the closet and lose myself again and again. I longed to be there. I craved the feeling of pouring my soul into a story.

A few days later, I went back into the closet and read over what I wrote. It was like I was in a dream when I wrote it. It didn't feel real.

> *With the first crack of the belt, she gasps for air, ears glued*
>
> *to the wooden door.*
>
> *"Didn't I!"*
>
> *Tears streamed down her cheeks, her head shaking with*
>
> *disbelief.*

My jaw dropped as I read each gripping sentence.

> *"Lord, please!" She prays. "Please don't let him*
>
> *kill my son!"*

I couldn't believe it. Those words could not have possibly have come from me. I was not that powerful. I wasn't a writer. I was a poet.

"Babe," I yelled, running from the closet. "Can you read this?"

I needed him to read it. I needed him to tell me this was real. That I, Khadija, had really written a story that good.

He sat down with me in the closet and read it. He swallowed deeply, he gasped, and by the time he was done, he looked at me with such belief in me and said, "Babe. You need to finish this."

I laughed. "I can't finish it. I have no idea how to do that. I'm a poet. My teacher would ask me to write a short story, and I would cringe. I can't -

"You can. I know you can. Whatever you did to get this, just keep doing it. I don't care if you have to have a nightmare every night, I'll hold you. This is good, and I don't even like to read."

His words lifted my soul. Maybe he was right. For the next couple of weeks, I did just that. I woke up at the crack of dawn, and I sat down in that dark closet, me and heaps of clothes, both dirty and clean and I wrote. I made up the characters as I went, living and talking to them as they went through the most difficult situations in their lives. I created a back story, motivations and drive. I couldn't wait to tell my mother. I had finally found my purpose.

Chapter Thirty Five

I went up to the hospital, just knowing my mother would be woke. I was feeling really good about telling her that I was on to something and that it felt right. For the first time in my life, it seemed I was going in the right direction. I was going down the path I wanted to go down.

I walked into her room. I stood by her bed, and I watched her once again do nothing. My heart grew a little heavy again. All the joy I had before walking in began to seep from my spirit, until I got just a little closer. My mother had the headphones on. Half of it was hanging off her head. I could hear our pastor preaching.

He was preaching about Job. I sat down, and I listened with her. It brought me back to the old days. The days, I couldn't really understand what the preacher was talking about, but in Sunday school, as I colored the biblical stories, I knew exactly what it meant to be Job, to be relentless, no matter what the devil threw in front of you.

I slid the headphones back onto her ear. I went back to my closet. I wrote.

I did this in cycles. I would visit my mother, listen to whatever sermon or album my brother had put on for her and then go back and pour back into my characters. They would have trials and tribulations just like Job, my mother and even I, but they would be resilient. I wrote:

"It's a rat. A rat!" Amina shouts out. Immediately, everyone in the auditorium turns their head, including Sam. An old woman with a cane almost breaks her neck to get down the aisle. Sam's feet are up by her chest as she watches people scramble from their seats and head to the exit. The director comes running over.

"What's wrong? What happened?" She asks.

"My apologies. I thought I saw something," Amina says with a smile and a nod.

Amina sits back down while the director walks away shaking her head.

"Did you see that?" Amina says. "If you really believe that there is a rat, a fire or anything dangerous, you will run. Even if you can't see it, all you have to do is believe it. Once you run, everyone else will believe you because you are taking action. It might take a while for people to follow you, support you, because maybe they are a bit slow. Maybe they have experienced false alarms, so it takes them a while to get past their own doubts, but you keep going.

Eventually, you will have the whole building behind you - If you believe it. You can't sit here and tell me one thing, try to sell me a dream, go back home, and sit on the couch and do nothing. That's not someone who believes. That is someone who dreams.

Now, what are you going to do about your situation?"

I couldn't wait to read my mother a piece of my work. At first, I was reading her favorite books to her, Danielle Steele, but now I had my own. I knew she would be proud.

I printed a couple of sheets off and went back up to the hospital. I read over it a dozen times as I waited for the elevator to take me to the third floor.

"She moved! She moved!"

I had just stepped off the elevator when I saw my mother's best friend running to the waiting room. She was in tears, she was shaking and everyone was so stunned, they just stared at her.

"She squeezed my hand," her friend said. "I'm telling you. I told her to squeeze, and she did!"

Goosebumps rose from my arms. I was scared. I was excited. I wanted to run into my mother's arms. My brother and sister and some other family and friends sprang up and ran into the room. I wasn't too far behind them. I wanted to know. I needed to see. Did my mother finally wake up?

I got into the room, but it was crowded. Everyone wanted to see a miracle. Everyone wanted to witness the impossible. I shoved my way to the front. I stood there. I waited.

The doctors studied my mother. They examined her vitals. One placed his finger inside her palm and said, "Dorothy. If you can hear me, squeeze my finger."

We waited. I held my hand over my mouth. My heart went wild, and my stomach hurt. The anxiety was killing me. Everyone was quiet. No one wanted to miss it. I wanted to cry. I didn't want to breathe. The anticipation was killing me.

"Dorothy," he said louder. "If you can hear me, squeeze my hand."

We waited, each one of us, searching for any kind of sign.

"Nothing," the doctor said.

I exhaled.

"You must have mistaken the doctor said. It is common among patients who are in a coma. Sometimes they will move, but it is just nerves. They can even smile."

"No! I'm telling you," she shouted, as if she was in church and on the verge of a shout. "She heard me. I know my friend!"

I grabbed my mother's hand. My sister grabbed the other. "Ma! Ma!"

She did nothing.

My heart broke again. All night, we tried to get her to respond to us, but she wouldn't. We tried everything, her favorite Marvin Gaye songs, her favorite Gospel songs, but nothing woke her up. All the while the doctors were still pushing for us to give up. It would only be fuel to my fire. I went back to my closet, and I kept writing. I wrote:

Bang. Bang. Bang.

"Give me the keys. Give me the damn keys," the man yells at Courtney.

Sam listens to her stepmother scream behind her bedroom door, begging for him to stop, for him to leave her daughter alone. She stares at the golden padlock on the door.

Sam tries to remain calm, while sitting at the edge of her bed. She can't stop her heart from pounding so hard. Her body is becoming tenser, her breaths deeper and her limbs freezing up. However, it doesn't take long for her body to no longer allow her to ignore the danger. Her heart is beating too fast and she is on the verge of tears. She is even more fearful that at any moment somehow, someway, the man is going to burst through the door.

I am strong. I am strong. I am strong because my momma said so. I am strong because my grandmother was strong. My great grandmother was strong. I will always be strong.

"No! Leave her alone," Courtney yells even louder.

Sam slams the journal down onto her bed and then runs into her dark tiny closet.

I exhaled, closed my laptop and in the morning I jumped back in that closet with Sam and I kept writing.

Six weeks later, I had finished my entire story. I was proud. I had my characters, David and Sam and they were just as alive and real as me.

But would anyone else love it?

Would anyone else care about my work, my characters, my world?

I didn't think so. But once again, my husband sat in the closet with me and assured me I was tripping. "You are an amazing writer," he told me. "Why don't you let someone else read it."

"No! I couldn't do that."

"People are going to tear it apart. Imagine how horrible that would feel? I don't want to go through that."

"Just do it. You never know."

A couple of days later, I put my first chapter on a website. This website was a place where anyone could post their stories for the world to see, to comment on, and frankly to love or hate. I posted it and waited. Each day went by with no response. It tugged at my heart. There were millions of people on there, yet not one person read my story.

"See," I said. "I must not be that good. Nobody but you like it for real."

"Be patient," he said. It's only been up there for a week."

Just a few days later, I got my first comment. "This is one of the best openers I've ever read. So powerful. WOW. I love it!"

Next comment from another stranger, "Whoa. I can't wait to see what happens next. That was awesome," The reader said.

The comments flooded in. The reads shot through the roof and then my story was chosen to be featured on the site. I couldn't believe it. All I could do was thank God for confirmation.

"Told you," Kimani said. "You don't ever want to listen to me. It always takes someone else to tell you something before you believe me."

"Nah uh," I said, knowing he was right.

I went back into that closet and poured my heart and soul back into the story. I wanted it to be longer. I wanted it to be better. I needed it to impact the reader. I needed more raw stories. I pulled from stories my husband would tell me. He would always start with, "I remember."

"I remember one time when I was a little kid, I walked to the corner store for a Moon Pie. I forgot how in the world I'd gotten the money, but I felt rich, and I had swag about myself because I was about to go ham on that marshmallow pie. I walked in and saw Donald."

As he was telling me the story, I closed my eyes and walked with him. I walked to the corner store all the time, and I remembered what it was like. I remember what it felt like for my thin soled Keds to hit the concrete sidewalk. I remembered looking up at the bright neon lights that said, 'Budweiser,' the sign that reassured me my mother's food stamps were good there and the smell of the winos walking out the store gripping the neck of their malt liquor. And the bell. I could always remember that bell that alerted the cashier to be aware of a new customer.

I placed myself there. I was the little girl walking behind him, watching his every turn down the aisle as he searched high and low for the pie - the anticipation of him finding it.

I then remembered my grandmother and how she'd sneak me a couple of dollars and send me to the store. "Tell them I sent you. Give them this money right here, and they'll throw in some chew." I had no idea what chew was, how illegal it was for a child to purchase chewing tobacco, but she'd given me enough to buy a bag of Funyuns and Red Pop, so I didn't care. I would never forget what it felt like to do something as simple as walk to the corner store anticipating walking back with some kind of sugar or chips in my hand. So as my husband poured into me his story, I was able to connect the dots. I was able to pull from my experiences and add in details here and there to form a complete scene.

"So, I'm at the cash register and I see him pull out this wad of money," he said.

"For real?" I said, as I took notes in my head.

"Yeah."

Kimani continued. "I looked up at him and watched him pull out a wad of twenties from his pocket. He looked at me, gave me a twenty and then told me I could get anything I wanted in the store. I thought I was rich for a second."

"Did he say something to you? Did you know he was a drug dealer?" I asked.

"Hell yeah, I knew. And I knew I wanted to be like him. I wanted the gold chains, the rims, the old school car on Daytons, the sounds - I wanted what he had and by the time I walked out the store, rushing to see him turn his engine, and turn up his sounds, I made up in my mind that once I got a few years older, I knew exactly what I wanted to do."

The man who gave Kimani that twenty-dollar bill, had just birthed KG. That motivation and desperation for the things a little boy never had, a way for him to change his circumstances overnight, that power he'd never felt before, I used all that, and I created a new phase in my character's life.

I picked up the phone. The first person I wanted to tell was my mother. I wanted to tell her that I had found the very thing I wanted to do for the rest of my life. I wanted to show her what I had written, that

I had finally stuck to something. I wanted to hear her say how proud she was of me. I put the phone back down. It was all a fantasy. She couldn't answer.

A few hours later, the phone rang.

"Dee!" my brother yelled. "Mom woke up!"

CHAPTER THIRTY SIX

I was speechless. I just kept listening to him and everyone shouting in the background at the hospital.

"Don't play," I said.

"God is good, Khadija. Mommy woke up!"

I was in tears. I knelt down. I closed my eyes and I thanked God. "Thank you! Thank you! Thank you!" I yelled.

I put the phone back up to my ear. "You mean she really woke?"

"Come up here and see!"

"Babe! We gotta get to the hospital," I yelled.

"What's wrong?" he said.

"My momma woke up!"

I couldn't get to the hospital fast enough and everything under the sun was going through my head. *What would I say to her? What would she say to me?*

I cried tears of joy.

I ran into the hospital, my feet moving so fast I almost slipped a couple of times. I didn't take the elevator, I took the steps. I needed to see her. Words could not describe the joy overflowing in my heart. "My mother is woke!"

"Ma!" I shouted as I rushed into her room.

I got inside and her room was once again crowded with people.

"Mommy!" I yelled. I pushed my way through the crowd. She was sitting up. She was fighting with the nurses as they were trying to pull the tubing out her throat.

227

"You woke up!"

She looked at me. She smiled. She couldn't talk, but she could mouth words. *You're here.*

Tears streamed down my face as I nodded. "I love you mom!" I said.

I blew her air kisses until they filled the room. I grabbed her hand as soon as the nurses would let me touch her. I didn't want to let go.

I love you, too! She mouthed.

We had church in that ICU room and we took it all the way back into the ICU waiting room. Everyone knew what God we served by the time we got done praising him.

"God is good!" someone would say.

"Yes, he is!" everyone shouted back.

"She still has a brain injury and will need therapy and..." The doctors seemed to never want to let up. The nurses were different. They were there every step of the way. They were in there crying too. It was a celebration. No one wanted to hear the odds anymore. She was living proof that God was real.

"I don't care! My mother woke up!" I said.

My mother stayed in rehabilitation for a month before they sent her home. She suffered a brain injury, but I was just happy she was still with us.

"Mom," I said, two years later. "I published my first book."

"You did?"

"Yep."

She looked at me the way she used to back in the day when she was proud of me. Her light shined bright. "What is it called?"

"*The Influenced*," I said.

She smiled even harder. "Wow. You are doing what you said you were going to do."

"Yeah. But I want to thank you, mom. Thank you for doing everything you could to make sure I would be successful in life. We fought, we had our differences, but mom, now that I have children of my own, I know you did it all out of love. I know some of the things that happened to you when you were younger and I know you really was just trying to protect me. You are so strong. All I want to do is make you proud, mom."

She looked at me and then hugged me tight. She seemed to have more strength since getting out of the hospital. "You already make me proud."

"No, mom," I said. "I want you to know that everything you invested in me was not in vain."

"But you are already wrote a book."

"I know," I said.

THIS IS ONLY THE BEGINNING.

LETTER FROM THE AUTHOR

*W*riting *my story in just eight weeks was surprisingly one of the hardest things I have ever endured.* It was not the deadline itself, but it was the pain I had to face, sentence by sentence, scene by scene, reliving moments I chose to hide that made it more difficult. However, where there is pain, there is healing. Writing my story happened to be the most transformative accomplishment I have ever experienced in my life. Even still, this book was really written for you.

I wrote *Dear Mom, I Hate You* for those who came to my book signings and asked, "How do I write my story? I need the world to hear me. *Girl, If you only knew what I've been through. My life is a lesson.* How do I write it? Where do I start? What is the next step after the manuscript is complete? How do I publish it?"

It was difficult for me to teach it without first writing my own story, so I set out to do just that. I am so grateful I did.

While writing my story, I wrote the Writer's Edition called, *Between The Lines.*

In this book, I give you the blueprint I used to write and publish *Dear Mom, I Hate You.* While writing my own memoir, I journaled the exact steps I took to write not just a book, but a powerful story. My mission is for you to write a story so impactful, it heals you and impacts the lives of others. If you ever wanted to write your own story or know someone who desires to finally get their story out, *Between The Lines* is definitely for you.

"I may not leave my children with fame or fortune when I depart from this Earth, but I can and will leave a legacy."

JOIN THE MOVEMENT

If *Dear Mom, I Hate You* has impacted you in a special way, I would love for you to join our exclusive community, Khadija Grant's Exclusive Fan Club.

It is a community of my most loyal fans in the world. It means you've read my books, shared my work, and shared a passion for the mission. It means I listen to you and add personal value to your own life goals.

Our community shares their passion by writing reviews, blogging, tweeting, and spreading the word about my influential books to their friends and relatives. It truly is a partnership and one that's based on the dedication we share to impact the world through storytelling.

If this is you, I hope you consider joining our private group on Facebook @KhadijaGrantsExclusiveFanClub

For more books and information visit

Khadijagrant.com

SPECIAL PREVIEW

THE INFLUENCED

CHAPTER ONE

The door slams shut. Wham! And the force of the door sends chills down her spine. Tara closes her eyes. That's all she can do. She has absolutely no control now. As if the slamming of the bathroom door isn't enough, she hears the lock turn. Click. Shutting her out of the room that she is so close to, yet feels so far away from.

"Lord, please!" she prays. "Please don't let him kill my son."

Wh-tsh!

With the first crack of the belt, she gasps for air, ears glued to the wooden door.

"Didn't I!"

Wh-tsh!

"Tell you to…"

Wh-tsh! Wh-tsh! Wh-tsh! Wh-tsh!

Tears stream down her cheeks, her head shaking with disbelief.

Wh-tsh! Wh-tsh! Wh-tsh!

The sporadic cries of pain escaping her son's mouth weaken her body. She clings to the door as if it's holding her up. What have I done? I should do something. I'm his mother.

Wh-tsh! Wh-tsh!

Tara's heart drops. She clenches her fingers into a fist.

Wh-tsh! Wh-tsh! Wh-tsh! Wh-tsh!

"Stop moving!" he yells with a deep growl.

Wh-tsh!

There is a change in the young boy's cry. Before, Tara could count on a yelp after each slash. Now there is only the hiss of the belt whipping through the air, across his skin, the shallow breaths seeping from his tiny lungs, no screams, just air. She waits and prays. She holds on to his last cry. It is her only proof that he is still alive.

Wh-tsh! Wh-tsh!

"Thomas, stop!" Tara screams, banging on the door as if it'll budge.

"Stop!" Panic takes over. She drops, knees crashing to the white tiled floor. She crouches down, clasps her hands together and prays, "Stop him. Please stop him."

Wh-tsh!

Tara presses her fingers into her temples, rubbing off the sharp pain in her head. Just the thought of the kindness and the joys of childhood being stripped from her son and being replaced with hate, anger, and resentment force more tears to trickle down her face. She knows all too well the everlasting affects of being beaten until you give up, beaten until you conform to whatever it is your mother, father or "man" wants you to become.

"Now, I bet you won't do it again!" Thomas warns one last time as he lands the last whip across David's back.

Tara hears a loud thump inside the bathroom, her son's body dropping to the floor. She gasps, her body rigid and stricken with fear.

Suddenly, she too falls into the bathroom as Thomas yanks the door open. She glances up at his broad shoulders and thick build. He is hovering over her trembling body. "What are you looking at?" he says. He stares at her, until her eyes fall to the cold bathroom floor. He steps over her, making sure his foot bumps into her shoulder.

Tara watches him grab a glass of lemonade out of the refrigerator, lie down on the couch in the living room, prop his legs on the ottoman and form a sick smirk. The only thing missing in Thomas's world is the jewel encrusted crown and beautiful half-naked women around him dangling fresh grapes over his lips.

As she stares at him, more chills surge through her body. She doesn't know if it's from the sudden draft sweeping cold air through the house or from the hate she feels toward him. She crawls to her son. David's legs are stretched across the floor, head resting on the blue rug that's nestled in front of the toilet. She lifts his head and examines his body. He is naked with only a damp, brown bath towel covering his thigh. Droplets of soapy water and sweat cover him, his tiny chest jumps, his lungs struggling to return to their natural rhythm.

Tara holds him while her eyes scan his body. They stop at the emerging bruises and blood that has oozed its way to the surface. "I'm so sorry, baby. I'm so sorry," she chants, sniffing and wiping tears from her face. She rocks him back and forth.

David tries to nestle in his mother's arms, but it only brings more agony. His teeth clench down on his bottom lip, but it's no match to the pain that's throbbing along his lower back, his thighs, arms, and legs. Staring at the wall, he imagines himself bigger, older and able to fight back. He dreams of the day his mother gets a job, packs up her bags and leaves his father. That was her promise to him, her excuse she gave him years ago, the reasons why she can't leave just yet. In his dream, she is smiling because she can finally live on her own. It's these thoughts, these bursts of hope that help him to endure such violent whippings. Slowly, his mind eases back into reality. He opens his mouth and struggles to force out the words with each hiccuping breath. "Ma-mee, I di-dn't br-eak it."

"Shh. I know, baby. I know." Wishing that somehow the whole incident could be undone, Tara rocks David, and replays the incident in her head:

It was mid-afternoon. The air conditioning had just kicked in, startling Tara and reminding her to check the time. When she glanced at the ticking hands and read the clock, her heart sped up.

"Dammit. I forgot. It's Tuesday," she said, "Thomas comes home early today." Snatching the broom from the corner of the kitchen, she scrambled to sweep the floor. As she swept, she'd use her free hand to fluff the brown couch pillows, use her knee to align the end tables and examined the room for anything out of place. She quickly brushed the last bits of trash into a pile, making sure not to leave even a crumb behind.

But as Tara bent down to grab the dust pan, the broom slipped out of her hand. A rush of air passed her head, followed by a crash. She jumped back. "Shit!" At first she was relieved that it didn't smack her in the head, but when her eyes caught a glimpse of the shattered trophy, she covered her mouth and whispered, "Oh no!" Seeing Thomas's only trophy clumped up in pieces in the midst of dirt and dust, her body stiffened. "He is going to kill me!"

She sat pieces of it up, trying to measure the damage. The tube of superglue was in one hand and two of the biggest broken pieces in the other. She shook her head at the two fragments of glass. There was no saving it. She placed the pieces back on the mantle and yelled for David to get in the tub. Singing to herself to calm her nerves, Tara wished that Thomas's anger management class – the one mandated by the courts – would help her. She sang the words to a gospel hymn from her childhood. "Glory, glory, hallelujah…" She hummed and silently prayed.

Within minutes, Thomas's footsteps stopped at the front door, the keys clashed against the metal knob, causing her breaths to shorten. She clenched her jaw while twisting the soapy cloth around in the glass cup, praying he wouldn't see the broken trophy, hoping he was in a good mood. She wrestled with her thoughts. Maybe I should have hid it. No, he would have noticed it being gone anyway. I should have been more careful. I know better.

She followed the sound of his heavy footsteps around the living room and when they paused, she took in a deep breath. "What the fuck?" she heard him say.

Squeezing her eyes like a child blocking out the anticipation of a scary monster, a boogeyman popping up from thin air, her thoughts ran wild. The fear in her heart was real; she'd thought the worst and it came true. The boogeyman, the scary monster, had just stepped right in the doorway of the kitchen, breathing deeply and waiting for an explanation.

"What happened to my shit?" Thomas yelled. He stood there holding a piece of the molded glass.

Tara didn't look up. Her eyes stayed fixed on the suds that were popping and the dirty cups that were bobbing up and down in the dish water.

"David, he…uh. He was bouncing the basketball," she stuttered.

Thomas didn't allow her to finish. He turned from the kitchen and stomped through the hallway to find David.

"David!" he yelled, first opening the boy's bedroom door. "Daaavid," he said as if playing a game of Hide and Go Seek.

Still in the kitchen, washing and rinsing the dishes, Tara listened while Thomas opened and closed doors. Her heart sped up as she waited.

"Yes, Dad?" David said, so childlike, so ignorant of the situation.

Tara tiptoed to the hallway with suds still running down her hand. She could see Thomas hold up the broken pieces and give David a piercing stare. She stood there, silent, as David lowered his head to his chest. Not a word came from his mouth. He fiddled around the water for his cloth and waited. I've got to tell him the truth. I can't. Tara put her head down and walked back to the kitchen.

Tara looks down at the marks spread across her son's body. It takes her mind back to the movie Roots. The similarities blow her mind. Images of Kunte Kinte being stripped down to his bare skin and being ruthlessly whipped until his will breaks engulfs her sanity. It brings chills to her body, makes her stomach nauseous and her heart pound. She can only think of one difference. Instead of being whipped by his master, her son was lifted up with one hand, his legs fighting the air, by a man that looks much like him - his father. It's a scene that she is all too familiar with, even as a child herself.

"I'm sorry, baby," Tara whispers, wishing that those words could lighten the load of guilt her heart carries. She wipes the tears from her cheek and licks the salty residue from her lips. "We are going to get out of here. I promise. We are going to get out of here," and with a soft touch, she smoothes her fingers along her son's arm to calm him.

A shallow knock against the glass portion of the screen door echoes through the house.

"Can David come out?" Daniel, the neighbor's kid, yells through the screen. Thomas eyes the little boy who is bending the flimsy screen with his head as he leans in to get a closer look inside.

"No, he cannot!" Thomas yells back. "And get off my damn screen."

☙

"What's wrong, Daniel?" his mother asks.

"David can't come out. He never gets to come out," Daniel says.

"Well, maybe he's busy."

Sheri glances at her son, who is still dressed in his school clothes – a crisp blue button down, khakis, and a pair of brand new loafers. She forces a weak frown. "Maybe I'll go over there tomorrow and see if he can ride with us to school."

Dressed in a knee length skirt with a flowered baking apron on,

Sheri kneels down to her son and stretches out her arms. "Come here. Give your mother a nice big hug." She squeezes him tightly and then kisses him on his round forehead. "Mommy loves you."

"Okay, Mom," Daniel says, pulling away from her. "I'm not a damn baby."

"Well, you are my baby," she responds. "Come. Help me set the table."

Daniel rolls his eyes, but helps anyway. He carries the ceramic bowls filled with whipped garlic mashed potatoes, creamy gravy, and steaming green beans to the table. He then places each dish in its proper position and waits for his mother to bring out the rest.

Sheri pulls out the china and silverware, and as her husband walks through the front door, she is pulling the garlic bread out of the stainless steel oven. The aroma of herbs, butter and garlic fill the room.

"Sorry I'm late," her husband says in a hurry. "I'm starving."

The athletic man unbuttons his police jacket, revealing his bright white t-shirt and thick muscular arms, and slings it along the couch. He rubs his cold hands together and loosens his belt.

From the draping tablecloth to the freshly polished wooden chairs, everything is arranged as if they are expecting company. Even the utensils are set properly - perfectly aligned - allowing them to easily work from the outside in. As a family, they stretch their hands out while Jacob leads prayer. "Lord, thank you for the food. Amen." From the knives slicing through the ham and the forks trying to stay in position, but sliding across the plates, it sounds like a band of violins are in dire need of a tuning.

"I had to respond to a last minute call," Jacob says, passing the gravy bowl to Daniel. "A man was stoned, running around in and out of traffic, naked." He chuckles in disbelief. "And this was after he assaulted a woman in the thrift store - you know, the one just off of 123rd and Broadway."

Jacob pauses for a second to take a big bite out of his swollen honey dinner roll. "That damn crack," he says in the middle of a chew.

"Crack? What's crack?" Daniel asks. His eyes light up, his voice heightens.

"Nothing," Sheri blurts. "It's nothing for you to worry about."

Daniel sighs. "You never want to tell me anything," he mumbles.

"Crack is a substance that people ingest into their bodies to escape the real world," his father says, smiling at him. "It's a bad drug that will destroy your life. It not only affects the addict's life, but the community suffers, the kids with parents in jail suffer, the mothers who are on the corner selling their —"

Sheri interrupts. "Enough about work." She signals Jacob to hush while eyeing Daniel's fully focused and excited stare.

"So, how has your day been going, honey?" Jacob asks.

"Great! Today I met with Daniel's teacher. I wish you could have been there. His teacher talked so highly of him. He is especially doing well in science and is sure to move on to middle school. Our son is going to be a doctor one day, right Daniel?" She glances at him in admiration.

"Right."

After dinner, Sheri tells Daniel to take a shower, and then, as if he is still a toddler, she reads him a bedtime story. She tucks him in and gives him yet another kiss on his forehead.

"Goodnight, Sweetie."

She flips off the light switch and smiles back at her son whose face is glowing from the baseball lamp positioned next to his bed.

∞

"Jacob, I don't know about our neighbors," Sheri says while lying down next to her husband in her flowered silk kimono. "I think something is going on with that poor little boy."

"What neighbors? What boy?"

"The ones that just moved next door. You know, the ones on Section 8."

Jacob nods. "Okay?" he says sarcastically.

"Their son always looks sad. He is never allowed to come out of the house. I don't think they like us very much," Sheri adds.

"Well, they are probably keeping to themselves," Jacob says, adjusting his pillow behind his head.

Sheri twists her lips like she just bit into a lemon. "I don't know about that, dear," she says, rubbing her fingers along Jacob's chest hair. "I'm telling you, the way they dress him, as if they don't own a washer and a dryer, they should be grateful he has a clean cut friend like our Daniel. He could be a great role model, you know." She stops to imagine her son helping the raggedy looking boy straighten up his image. She smiles at her brilliant idea. "You know what? We have some leftover ham in the refrigerator. I should have Daniel—"

Suddenly, a loud ring echoes throughout the house. It's the phone. Jacob slings the covers from his waist and jumps out of bed. Sheri crawls out of bed, tiptoes to the doorway, and stretches out her neck as far as possible to hear every word that comes tumbling out of Jacob's mouth.

"Hello? Hi, Dad!" Jacob says to his father on the phone. He leans on the refrigerator, taking shallow breaths to slow down his breathing.

"No. I told you his birthday is on the 14th, not the 7th," Jacob explains. "It's next weekend."

Jacob shakes his head.

"Oh! I knew that!" Jacob's father says so loudly through the phone, the neighbors could probably hear him. "I haven't been feeling well lately. I was really calling to let you know that I am unable to make it to see him for his birthday. What are your plans?"

Jacob rests his forehead on the counter and takes in another deep breath. He controls his tone to hide his irritation. "Oh, nothing big, just a small get-together."

His father quickly chimes in. "Listen, I will deposit some money into Daniel's account sometime tomorrow." Jacob lifts his head from the counter so fast his head starts spinning. "So get whatever you need, all right?"

"Dad, why do you always insist on paying for things?" Jacob tries to stop the big smile from affecting his voice. "The go-kart, the big screen TV, hell, everyone in the neighborhood is going to think we're rich."

His father lets out a laugh, but a series of dry coughs interrupt it. "That never stops you from going to the bank, son, now does it?" He pauses to cough again. "Just get the boy something nice. I feel terrible that I can't make it."

After hanging up the phone with his father, Jacob's breaths settle. His heart immediately thumps with anticipation. He nervously combs his fingers through his black stringy hair, and while nodding his head, he ponders for a second, I wonder if Sheri heard him. He softly snaps his fingers. I should have gone down to the basement.

Jacob eases his way back into the bedroom and walks straight into their bathroom; he can feel Sheri's eyes following him every step of the way. His body tenses up, his heart speeds up, but he is trying to act normal. Not too excited, but not too relaxed. He's anticipating at least three grand. He bites down on the smile that's forming. I'll have enough to throw Jacob a nice party. That will get Sheri off my back. And have a little bit left over for…"

❧

Tara smacks the jumping alarm clock on her nightstand, trying to deaden its tired and worn out sound. "Damn, it's too early in the morning for this shit," she complains. She forces the thick comforter back over her head. She lies there on a bed of Thomas's curly chest hair and tightens her squeeze around him. *He is going to change. I know it,* she thinks.

Her mind takes her back to the wild night they shared just before the sun went down. Images of Thomas's strong hold around her waist as he moaned and groaned, the strength he used to pull her body every which way he wanted to, pulling her hair back and the sweet whispers in her ears are flashing through her mind. Goosebumps are forming, growing on her arms just thinking about it. It puts a smile on her face. "I know he loves me," she whispers as she gets lost in her thoughts. She looks up at Thomas. He's sleeping so peacefully, barely even making a sound. A bigger smile grows on her face.

The beaming sun peeking through the curtains remind her of the time. Tired, exhausted, and even sore in some areas of her body, she drags herself to her feet. She glances at the two tall bottles of Belvedere and the stack of unopened bills beside them. *What am I going to do if he can't find another job? I'm not moving back to the Projects. I don't care what I have to do.* She takes in a deep breath and shakes her head. *Why does my life have to be so damn hard?*

"Wake up, D! Wake up!"

Tara slings the covers from David's bruised body and smacks him on his butt. He doesn't move, so she whacks him again. With his eyes still closed, David just lies there. The first hit had woken him up, but he continues to lie there to get a few more minutes of sleep.

"You better not miss that bus," Tara says, trying to clear the sleep from her voice.

David gradually opens one eye. Whack. She hits him again.

"Okay. I'm up," he says, jumping down from the wooden bunk bed.

"Make sure you wear long sleeves, you hear."

"Yes, ma'am."